A 7 step process to creating your best life

THE
FOUR
MINUTE
MINUTE
FORMULA

EDDIE SLOWIKOWSKI

I dedicate this book to my 4 children: Jack, Gracie, Adeline & Molly. Being your Father has been the most rewarding, fulfilling and amazing experience of my life. It is the most important thing I have ever or will ever be. The fact that you are here is proof that sometimes our Dreams really do come true! You have each in your own unique way given my life its most beautiful moments, its deepest purpose and its most profound experience of Love. I am so abundantly proud of you & I Love you with all my Heart and Soul!

You are Magnificent!!!

-Dad

&

To Diane…My Sunshine!!!

I could not and would not be the Man I am today without you in my life. More than anyone, you've shown me how to be my best and the love I feel for you is simply eternal! Thank you for loving me! I am the luckiest Man alive to have you as my partner in life.

-Eddie

INTRODUCTION

It was that same feeling I've had countless times through the years as a competitive runner: Nervous, excited, scared. I was used to it. It came with the territory. The race was just a few hours away yet those feelings were what woke me on this morning. Today was a big day. It's not everyday you have a shot at the realization of a dream. When we entered the Armory at Boston University the musty smell of an ancient structure hit me. This building had been around forever. This was the site of what many believed to be the fastest indoor track in the country! The corridor was dimly lit and the sound of water dripping somewhere in the darkness created an ominous feel. We came upon some big old steel doors as my Coach said, "step aside" and without hesitation pushed with ferocity as the doors sprang open. Suddenly the dark corridor was bathed in light as we entered a huge cavernous indoor facility. In the center was the track. We approached the track almost reverently because we had heard the lore of the incredible races that were had on that old wooden relic that lay before us.

As we stepped on the wooden track it had a very familiar feel to it. It was just like the one me and my teammates built back at Loyola University Chicago a few years earlier. This track had that bounce to it and the turns were banked almost identical to ours. As I ran, a smile came to my face and a surge of adrenaline shot thru my body for this felt like home. The nerves I was feeling were giving way to confidence with each stride I took. I was feeling good!

My Coach pulled me aside then said, "lets go over the game plan." We sat in the stands about 90 minutes before the race and methodically worked out exactly how this race should go. My teammate and very good 800meter runner, Andre Fomby had graciously agreed to be the "Rabbit" in the race even though he had a race coming up about 30 minutes after mine. The "Rabbit" is a runner that is designated to set the pace for the rest of the runners. They only run 1/2 the race but they lead you through to where you need to be if your goal is to run a certain time. The "4 minute mile" requires a nice even pace in order to run that fast over that distance. This indoor track was 8 laps to the mile so do the math, 30seconds a lap will get you 4 minutes. Obviously, the goal is to run just under that. Once the rabbit drops out, the rest of the runners need to take over. My coach had informed me that there was another great miler there that day that I needed to be aware of. His name was Paul Vandergrift from William & Mary College. He had run 4:01 the week before and he was hoping that this fast track could help him break that illustrious mark as well. I ran 4:03 a week earlier so I felt it would come down in the end to the two of us. I approached Paul and asked him if he wanted to work together. I told him that when Andre dropped out that I would be willing to take the 5th lap if he'd take the 6th lap? The last two laps would be "Every man for himself." He agreed to the game plan. Everything was in place and now all that was left to do was race!

The moments before they call you to the starting line are typically the most nerve wracking. Although you are ready to race, there is a nervous apprehension because you know that this will not be easy and that you will suffer. This is why distance runners are an "interesting breed" because they voluntarily set themselves up within a race to have to negotiate pain. It's in these precarious pre race moments that you try to calm your body and mind because you know the explosion of energy that will come at the start of the race is going to be intense. On this day, I felt pretty calm, confident and ready. The announcement came, "Attention, Attention Please... it is now time for the mile run and we need all milers to please report to the starting line." I put the final touches on my shoelaces making sure my racing flats were secure. I then stood and turned to make my way to the starting line, when out of nowhere my Coach appeared before me. He put his hands on my shoulders and with a reassuring smile he said, "This is it Eddie! You've done everything you've needed to do to prepare for this moment and I am so proud of you! Now its time to go out on that track and MAKE IT HAPPEN!" I gave a smile of my own and confidently headed to the starting line. As I took my spot on that starting line I thought about what my Coach said and I thought about his smile. That smile told me everything I needed to know, my Coach believed in me but now it was time for me to believe in myself! The starter raised his right arm, "Runners Take Your Mark...BANG!"

As the gun sounded, my body sprang into action. It's hard to describe that moment. A surge of pure adrenaline courses through your body in a matter of milliseconds and before the mind can catch up to what is happening the body has reacted. I shot off of that line as the runners to my left and right jostled for position. The plan was that Andre would immediately take the lead and my job was to get out right behind him. That's exactly what happened. The race had begun! As I followed the lead of Andre who needed to bring us out around 30 seconds, I found myself right up on his heels like a car tailgating to close on the highway urging you to speed up. Half way into that first lap I yelled to Andre, "Pick up the pace Dre, your not going fast enough!!!" I'll never forget Andre's response. He glanced over his shoulder at me and said in a very controlled voice, "Trust me Eddie, I got this." As we approached the first lap the pace felt slow and I was sure we were going to come thru at 33 or 34 seconds but as we crossed the line completing the first lap the official holding the timer yelled out, "28-29 seconds!" Andre was doing a perfect job pacing and I just needed to trust in him and know that he had my back. I've always had trouble giving up the control in life and it has actually been something that has hindered me and not helped so I began to calm down and trust in my teammate and follow his lead. (This is a precursor to living a better life.

3

We can't control it all. We shouldn't even try) Second lap, we were at 58 seconds and the 3rd lap 1 minute 28 seconds. Andre was doing a perfect job pacing and I was running as comfortably and confidently as I could, conserving my energy for the 2nd half of the race. Now we were coming up to the 1/2 mile point where we obviously needed to be at 2 minutes to be on pace and Andre brought us thru at a perfect 1:59! At the half, we were exactly where we needed to be. Andre had done a perfect job setting the pace and I felt good!

The 2nd half of the race had begun and it was my turn to take over the pacing. As the body slowly begins to tire you need to actually feel as though you are picking up the pace to stay consistent so that's what I did. I tried to keep it as even as I could so as not to expend too much energy to soon. At the 5th lap we needed to be at 2:30 to be on pace and I brought us thru at 2:29. I had done my job and now it was Paul's turn to take over so I drifted into lane 2 in order to allow Paul easy access to take over and lead us through the 6th lap. As I began to move into lane 2 coming off the banked turns I noticed my teammate, Marc Burns who was diligently watching the race and cheering me on sprinting across the infield of the track yelling something to me. I couldn't hear what he was saying until I came off the turn and was now running past him. With great ferocity Marc yelled, "Eddie, Paul's not there!!! He's not There!!! You're gonna have to do this yourself!!!"

Paul wasn't there, he was hurting and falling behind and was not able to take over the pace. In fact, no one was there with me but I hadn't noticed because I was out front and "in the zone" so focused on the task at hand. I had no clue that I was alone out front until my teammate made me aware. I'll never forget that moment and I'll never forget those words, "Paul's not there...You're gonna have to do it yourself!" One thing that became crystal clear in that moment was that as we all journey forth toward our personal goals and dreams, of course we need the help of other people. No one can do it alone. In everyone's journey though, there will be some definitive moments where it is you and your dream and the question comes down to: How bad to you really want it? What are you willing to do, what are you willing to sacrifice to make your life everything you hope and dream it could be? This was that moment for me! So I put my head down and headed back into lane one. I was going to have to take it the rest of the way by myself. The problem now was the pain had arrived. Yeah here it comes, the pain. It's inevitable because in every race you run as a distance runner, pain will always be part of the equation and its how we deal with this pain that will make or break us. This was my moment of truth.

As I approached the 6th lap, I needed to be at 3 minutes to be on pace and that's exactly where I was. I had just 2 laps to go and if I could run these last two laps in under a minute I could have my dream of breaking the "4 minute mile!" The final phase of the race was now upon me and the pain was intense. My legs are getting heavy and my lungs are starting to burn. I can feel my heart pounding in my chest and the body slowly shutting down. But this is why we train. This is why we put in all those miles, all those hours and all that sacrifice. The pain is now your companion and you simply cannot allow it to take over. One must live with it and try desperately to overcome it. 7th lap, I'm at 3:30! I've got one lap to go! Just one more lap! If I can run it under 30 seconds my dream will be real. It's so close I can taste it but I can also taste the bitterness of lactic acid forming in my muscles as the body struggles with the deprivation of oxygen. My legs now feel like led weights and my lungs are on fire! All I was thinking in that moment was: "Fight thru the pain!!! Fight thru It!!!" As I came off the final turn I remembered how important it was to get to that finish line. Push all the way thru the finish line! I pushed with everything I had digging deeper then ever before as I leaned toward the line! With no more breath in me I crossed the line and fell into my Coach's arms. I looked up at him and the first thing I noticed was his smile. He motioned for me to look at the trackside clock. It read: 3:58.62!!!

I did it! I broke the "4 minute mile!!!" The 169th American to do so! When my eyes locked on that clock a feeling came over me that was so pure and magnificent! The realization of what I'd done had suddenly made all those years of running, suffering and sacrifice worth it! This was an actual dream come true!

I have learned incredible things from that experience. I have discovered a "Blue Print" for Success and Peak Performance. From that race, from my years as a "World Class" runner and the decades that have followed as a Performance Expert Speaker, Consultant and Author I discovered a formula. I call it "The Four Minute Formula" designed for personal achievement and fulfillment that could apply to all things in life and help create real and lasting results. That is the goal and desire behind this book, to teach you this formula in hopes that it will bring you the life you've always hoped and dreamed of. This formula is designed to be easy to follow and it will create significant results when implemented. How do I know? Because I have been teaching this formula to fortune 500 companies, professional athletes, top-performing sales teams and Associations all over the country for the last decade. The "4 Minute Formula" is a 7-step process and here it is:

1. Define WHAT you want & WHY you want it.

2. You must BELIEVE that what you want is possible. Utilize the power of the mind & your Inner vision

3. Identify your team. Discover the people that will help you along the way.

4. Design & implement your game plan.

5. Prepare for the PAIN. Learn to Adapt & innovate while developing resiliency.

6. Set your "Destination Point."

7. Give back to our World. "BE OF SERVICE"

These are the 7 steps to the formula and now it's time to put them to work for you. We will break each one down in the following chapters so that by the end you will understand the Formula for YOUR BEST LIFE!

On your mark...Get Set...GO!!!

STEP #1:

DECIDE WHAT YOU
WANT & WHY

WHAT DO YOU WANT? You'd be amazed by how many people I work with who are looking for solutions but simply cannot answer that question. How do you know what to work towards if you cannot even define what you want? Knowing what you want however is simply not enough. You must also be clear on WHY you want it. Once you can identify these two things, then you can be on your way towards its realization. Can you answer those two vital questions? It all starts there. I opened this book with a very specific Goal/Dream in my life. I wanted to run a mile under 4 minutes. That is a very specific Goal/Dream. In fact, research proves that the more specific you are about what you want the more likely you are to achieve it. Remember though that this is just the first step. Knowing what you specifically want is imperative. Now you must answer, why do you want it?

I had the Goal/Dream of breaking the 4-minute mile the summer before my Sophomore year in High School. The reason was because I wanted to be a "World Class" runner. I wanted to be the best! I have always had a strong competitive drive and at that stage in my life, winning was all there was. If I could break the 4-minute mile then there would be no denying that I was GREAT! (It is fascinating the role the "EGO" plays throughout our lives)

The 4 minute mile became a highly sought after yet incredibly elusive feat in the world of competitive running around the time of World War 2. A couple of Swedish runners had lowered the world record to 401.4. Once the war hit, racing had come to a standstill. Breaking this barrier had captured the world's imagination. It was universally believed that this feat was literally impossible. In fact, Doctors and Scientists alike would claim that the human heart could not sustain that amount of exertion for that long. What they actually said was that the heart would "explode" under such intense stress. Although people started getting close, no one had ever been able to do it. It wasn't until 1954 when, of all people, a Doctor believed he could actually accomplish this without his heart exploding in the process.

The date was May 6th, 1954 at Iffey Road track in Oxford, England where Dr. Roger Bannister ran the first sub 4-minute mile in a time of 3:59.4 seconds! This was groundbreaking because what was once thought to be "impossible" was now possible. One of the most important outcomes of this milestone was now the "belief" that this could be done. In fact, 44 days later it was accomplished again. Then less then 2 months after that it was done again! The sub 4-minute mile became a thing of legends and it quickly became the dream of every aspiring middle distance runner. In 1983 it became mine.

THE STARTING LINE

I like to start with the end in mind. Where is this journey going to take you? Before a pilot hits the skies, they create the flight path for where they want to go. Knowing where you'd like to end up can help you know how to get started. Understanding why you want to end up there will give your goal/dream its purpose and meaning. This purpose gives your brain what it needs to provide the profound motivation required to maintain consistent action towards the realization of the goal/dream. This is key because you will face challenges along the way that can and most likely will derail you. Your "WHY" will keep you coming back. Let me give you an example of why your "WHY" is so important.

What if I asked you, "What percentage would you give yourself of making a million dollars legally in the next 12 months?" Most people say zero or 1% to 2% chance. But when I change the question to, "What percentage would you give yourself of making a million dollars legally in the next 12 months and if you don't your children will be killed?" Suddenly the answer changes to 100%. The major difference is the "Why" behind the answer, the "Motivation" to get it done! If this were the scenario, I believe that somehow you would find a way.

DO YOU BELIEVE IN MIRACLES?

I'll never forget the night of February 22nd, 1980. My Dad and I are sitting in the family room watching the Winter Olympics as the US men's hockey team was taking on the Soviets. The Soviet Union team was made up of a bunch of professionals while the US team, a bunch of college and a few high school amateur players. The Soviets were a powerhouse and they had won 6 of the last 7 gold medals in Olympic hockey and no one I mean no one had given the US team a chance in hell to win. But on this night, the US team believed and they played inspired, amazing hockey and as the clock ticked down to zero and the announcer Al Michaels exclaimed: "Do you believe in Miracles? YES!" The U.S.A Olympic Hockey team had won 4-3! It was a miracle! It was such an inspiring scene as my Dad and I went crazy, jumping out of our seats and cheering at the spectacle we had just witnessed! I'll never forget how my Dad just grabbed me in a huge embrace and yelled out, "WE ARE THE CHAMPIONS!" When we sat back down and watched the pandemonium and celebration continue on TV, my father turned to me and said, "Now that's the way to go thru life Son! You've got to be the BEST!!! You gotta be THE BEST!!! I was in eighth grade on that night and it had a huge impact on me. It made a lasting impression.

A year later I would be going into High School and I know my Father had high expectations for me. I was the 2x junior high school conference champion in Cross Country and my Dad could not wait to see what I'd do on the bigger stage of High School Athletics. Once high school began, my Dad was always on me to be THE BEST. To be the best in High School meant being the State Champion. So that became my goal. My Dad and I would argue quite a bit because he had a problem with my work ethic or lack there of. He wasn't the only one. My Coaches had a problem with me as did my older teammates. I was so lazy my freshmen year that the team gave me a nickname that stuck all the way thru High School. They called me "SLACKMAN" because I was without a doubt the laziest kid on the team and I was a "Slacker".

My Dad was an extremely hard worker and he would constantly say, "To be the best, you have to work for it. There is no substitution for dedication and hard work!" My Dad would come to all of my races and in my first year although I wasn't training very hard, I was winning all the freshmen competitions quite easily. I felt that no one could touch me. I believed I was the best. It wasn't until we had a cross country meet with York high school at their home course. I again won the freshmen race rather easily. I then watched the sophomore race and witnessed this kid from York named Jim White win that race rather easily. It wasn't until after the race that I was told Jim White was only a freshman. That moment is where the rivalry began. I always thought I was by far the best freshmen runner in the state, but after witnessing what Jim White was doing I quickly realized I had some strong competition.

As the next few years progressed I continued to dominate almost all my races. By sophomore year I was named All State in cross-country. By junior year I began to notice the emergence of some other highly gifted runners. Names like: Mark Deady, Steve Miller, Tom Bellos, Jon Vanscoyoc and of course, Jim White. I also began to understand the benefits of hard work and I became the hardest working member of the team. I was now "SLACKMAN" in name only. Once senior year rolled around all the names I mentioned had the ability be the state champion. My singular focus was to be the best, to be that champion. I wanted to make my Dad proud. I remember the pressure mounting as the big race approached and I remember my Dad continually harping on what it takes to be the best. He was on me quite a bit. By now, I was used to it. Once the championship season arrived I was running better than ever. I won the conference meet and then I won the regional meet. At sectionals I placed third which was good enough to qualify for State. All that was left was the State meet itself. I was ready!

Finally, the big day arrived. The IHSA State Cross Country Meet! I awoke to the Sun shining through the hotel window. It looked as though it was going to be a beautiful day. I was nervous, scared and excited all at the same time. The biggest race of my life was just a few hours away. After grabbing a light breakfast, our team loaded into the school van and we headed to Detweiller Park in Peoria, Illinois the official site of the IHSA Illinois State Cross Country Championships. As we drove, out of nowhere dark clouds started rolling in. It was beginning to look rather ominous. Then the thunder crashed and it started to rain. It was coming down like cats and dogs. The race officials huddled and decided that because there was no lightening that the race would go on. After slogging thru the warm up on the rain soaked course we all knew it was going be muddy and quite sloppy. No matter though, because everyone was in the same boat. We all had to run in it. As the runners convened on the starting line and the rain was still coming down. I stood there with about a thousand of Illinois' best runners and we were all about to take off heading in the same direction. An important key to doing well in a cross-country race is getting off to a good start. With so many runners, if you don't get out well and near the front you can get caught behind the sheer mass of humanity. If that happens, it becomes next to impossible to work your way thru to the front. I knew I had to get out fast. As the starter raised his pistol all things in my universe stopped and for a brief moment I heard my Fathers voice deep within say, "BE THE BEST!" And then, the gun went off!

As the rain continued I put my head down and bolted off the starting line. I ran as fast as I could thru the raindrops and before I knew it, I found myself in the lead pack with about 7 other runners. I looked around and noticed that it was the 7 best runners in the State. All those names I mentioned earlier. We were all keenly aware of each other and we all had the same goal, to be the State Champion. As we approached the one-mile mark I don't know what happened but something stirred inside of me. A little voice from deep within spoke to me saying, "It's time to go! Don't wait any longer and don't wait for anyone else! This is your race! Take it to them NOW!" At that very moment I took off and put in a surge. Before I knew it I had opened up a 10 yard lead on the pack! I kept pushing the pace and in a few more seconds it was 20 yards. As I looked over my shoulder I noticed only one guy coming after me and that one guy was Jim White from York High School. One thing you need to understand is that York High School has probably the greatest tradition of cross-country teams in the history of the United States and Jim White had been my biggest rival since freshmen year. He caught up to me and together we continued to push the pace. As we came upon the two-mile mark we had 50 yards on everybody else! With a mile to go we knew the championship was going to come down to either him or me. We continued pushing the pace and alternating the lead. We both knew that it was going to come down to the finish to determine the winner.

With about 1/4 mile to go I knew it was time to give it all I had and sprint to the finish. It was amazing how many fans were lining both sides of the course screaming and cheering us in but all I remember hearing was the beating of my heart and my breathing. At that moment I took my gloves off and threw them into the crowd and took off! The only problem was so did Jim White. We went neck and neck for about 100 yards until I noticed he was pulling ahead. He had a step on me, then two, then three. I dug down so deep giving it everything I could but on this day it just wasn't enough. Jim White finished first and I was runner up.

As I walked thru the finish line chute I felt so disappointed. I had come so close to being the best. I was upset not just because I had lost but because I knew I had let down my Father. When I emerged from the finishing chute the first person I saw off in the distance was my Dad running toward me. He was weaving in and out of people and knocking some out of the way just trying to get to me. As he got closer and his face came into focus I noticed his eyes were opened wide and he had this huge smile. He rushed to me, gathered me in his arms and without a word gave me the biggest hug of my life. I remember thinking in that moment, "Oh no! He didn't see the finish, he thinks I won." When he put me down I looked at him with sad eyes and said, "Dad, I lost. I got beat. I was second." Without missing a beat my Dad exclained, "I know! I saw the whole thing! What an incredible race! Son, you ran a fantastic race!" I was shocked and relieved all at the same time. He continued, "At the one mile mark when you took the race into your own hands and you just took off, that took such guts and courage! You were amazing! I was so proud of you! Today you didn't hold back and you went for it and you gave it everything you have! That's how you do it Son! I am so proud of you because today you did YOUR BEST!"

The words echoed in my mind: YOUR BEST! My Dad continued by saying that all he ever wanted from me was to do the very best that I could. Hard work and dedication was key and he wanted me to live that way but he just didn't know how to motivate me. He has always wanted me to be the best version of myself. It never meant being THE BEST it meant being YOUR BEST! My Dad knew that if I could figure out that one universal truth then I would do just fine in my life. To this day when I think about that memory it brings such warmth to my heart. I always thought while I was growing up that my Dad would not be satisfied unless I was #1, unless I was the champion. But I had it wrong. All we can ever ask of ourselves is to be our best. It never does anyone any good to compare themselves to others because we are each our own person. I was heard that comparing ourselves to others is the thief of joy. I couldn't agree more. We need to discover more and more how to be BETTER. I believe we have an idea of when we are striving to be or to do our best. I believe when we do, the world begins to benefit from it. It is time to get acquainted to the better versions of you and what you need to do to stay true to that person... it really is all we can ask of ourselves.

What I've come to find is that most people are not fully aware of who they are when they are being "Their Best." In order to achieve this it requires a mindfulness practice. When you take the time to envision the best version of who you are it is important to be as specific as you can. What exactly are you doing and what is going on within you that helps "create" this state of being? For example, how do you treat yourself? Sometimes we become so self-critical and the thoughts we have about who we are can be very negative. I firmly believe that we can only act upon and expand upon the thoughts we attach to. The thoughts we focus on become our living consciousness. If we find ourselves constantly seeing ourselves in a negative light, we will expand upon that and make negative choices that lead to negative outcomes. Sometimes we find ourselves in negative situations because we literally, through our choices put ourselves there. When a person habitually finds themselves in a "shit storm" where negative things seem to be happening all around them, I believe in many cases it's because deep down its what they believe they deserve and thus, they find a way to create it. It is the ultimate power of the unconscious. This is why the most important person you will ever LEAD in your life is YOU.

Leadership is not a noun. It is not a person place or thing. Leadership is a verb. It is action. Leadership is a decision on how you will conduct your life. The word decision comes from the Latin root which means to "cut off from." When we make a decision we cut off all other options and we begin to move in that direction. When we can't make up our minds or "decide" we can become stuck. I've met many people in my life who are simply stuck in the mud because they don't know what it is they truly want. This is why the most successful people you meet are also typically very decisive people. They know that nothing changes without ACTION. One might not always make the right decision but at any rate a decision itself promotes action, which promotes some type of creation. Some sort of result will come from each and every decision and action we take. It may not always be the result we hoped for but something gets created in the process. When searching for leaders you want to look for decisive people to be in key management roles. You want people who see and experience the organization or Team as an extension of who they are. You want their identity to at least in part be intertwined with the vision and values of the organization. These are the people who do not see a difference between their time and the organizations time. For them, time is of the essence to be used to fulfill the goals and the vision of the team regardless of how long it takes! When it comes to determining what you want, its leadership that helps bring it to action. Thus, we must first learn to effectively lead ourselves before we can lead others. Know what you want and determine in your heart why you want it. This is the first step, the launching point. When we know what we want we can begin the next steps to making it happen. We will begin to create it.

What do you want in your life?

Do you know what the most frequent response is that I get to the question, "What do you want in your life?" The answer is "Happiness." Did you ever notice that the things we hope for and dream about are at its deepest roots a desire to experience more happiness and well being in our lives? The problem is we have a hard time identifying or fully understanding what happiness is. Is it a state of being, an experience or a tangible thing? Is it a consciousness? Is it simply pleasure? If you look at pleasure itself it is contingent upon time, upon its object, upon the place. Pleasure is usually a temporary experience. That is why the truest experience of happiness has to be more about "well-being." A deeper way of looking at this is that "well-being" is not just a mere pleasurable sensation but rather a deep sense of serenity and fulfillment. It is something that actually underlies all emotional states and all the joys or sorrows that can come our way. This begs the question, "Can we have this well being while being sad?" Maybe we are looking into a different level of existence. Think of it like the Ocean. On the surface it can change drastically from a calm mirror like smoothness to stormy waves crashing and thrashing about but the depth is unseen and unchanging. It is still and serene beneath the surface. That depth can become our existence and our deeper experience of life. We don't always have to live on the surface where so much turmoil and chaos can occur at any moment. We can live within the depth that stays consistent and calm and peaceful. I believe Organizations and teams that thrive have that depth to them which underlies their true success. When I think about what I want in my life, what will help me live a better life, this sense of serenity, calm and peace are what I strive for and yet can be quite elusive.

Our pursuit of happiness seems to have become an acquisition of outer conditions in our lives. A gathering of things that we convince ourselves will bring about joy. The problem with this type of happiness is that like the surface of the ocean it can change in a heartbeat. We may lose something or not be able to acquire something. We may constantly want what we don't have. We may not be satisfied with what we do have. We begin to comparatively live our lives and look around and say to ourselves: "I do not have what someone else has and thus my life is incomplete." This is one of the down sides to social media. So many of us are "comparatively" living. In my estimation there is a lack of "authenticity" to many of the posts we see from others. Much of what we see feels manufactured. It's like people show you only their "highlight reel" of life. This begs the question, "How real is this?" This type of happiness is elusive and short lived. Is it possible to change our way of being to look into the depth of who we are and find our happiness? Of course it is possible but like anything worthwhile in life it won't come easy. It takes practice. It is imperative that we stop comparing ourselves to others and look within to our depths and find the true essence of what can bring us happiness and joy.

3 types of happiness:

1. Pleasure

2. Passion

3. Purpose

To help you determine "What you want and Why" make sure you apply the three P's:

PLEASURE: This is the most temporary experiences of happiness but can be the most intense. We need pleasurable experiences in our lives because it gives our existence its "Mojo!" (Remember when Austin Powers lost his MOJO and just wasn't the same?) Experts believe we have two major motivating factors in our lives. The first is the avoidance of pain but the 2nd is the experience of pleasure. Pleasurable experiences are what we live for. Researchers have shown that the brain's dopamine system is highly active when we experience pleasure. Dopamine has been thought of as the brain's "Pleasure Chemical." It's the release of this neurotransmitter in the nucleus accumbens, a cluster of nerve cells lying underneath the cerebral cortex. It is an essential part of the human experience. When trying to determine what you want and why, we need to ask ourselves, "Would the realization of this goal or idea give me pleasure?" If the answer is "YES" then try to determine in what way? When we can attach pleasure to the pursuit of our goals and dreams then we will be much more likely to commit to its realization and the work that goes along with it. Sometimes it feels good to simply feel good!

PASSION: In my mind PASSION is the fuel that gives us the energy to perform at peak levels. When we feel Passion in our lives it creates a fire behind our "WHY". When we can emphatically explain why we want to do something its usually because there is a deep emotional attachment to it. This is vital for it gives your daily life a deeper meaning. The people who in my estimation live extraordinary lives do so because they are extremely passionate about the life they lead. When you are trying to determine what you want in your life, ask yourself if you are passionate about it? How do you know? Is this something you would do for free? There are some endeavors in life that generate such passion that we'd find a way to experience it no matter what. Of the many PEAK PERFORMERS I have met in my life, one thing they have in common is PASSION! This passion will lead us directly to our third "P".

PURPOSE: Finally we hit the true "why" behind what we do: Purpose! One of the things that define our experience in such an impactful way is the purpose we feel throughout our lives. Our purpose is the framework for our identity. One important distinction in finding your purpose is to look at where you are in this moment of your life. The present will give you some indication of what you may be seeking. For no matter what path you may choose, know that it will lead right back to you in that new space and time of your life. The question becomes what do you want your journey to feel like along the way? Immerse yourself in living your life in the present. Act "as if" what you want is already within you. Try to fully grasp what it feels like to have what you say you want. Can you imagine what your life will feel like when that happens? Does it give your life more meaning and purpose? Does it bring you what you hope to feel? If it does, then I think you are on the right path. Breaking the Four Minute Mile gave me an understanding of a purpose that I didn't realize had always been there. That purpose was a knowing that I can do extraordinary things with my life! The deeper purpose I came to know deep within was what my Dad was trying to help me understand: Strive to do the best you can in all areas of your life! All we can ask of ourselves is this very thing and when we live our present in that mode our purpose becomes clear. For you are unique, there is no one in this world exactly like you! Therefore, who you are, your life already has purpose and meaning. Your voice needs to be heard in this world. Your actions need to be felt. For when it is, you cannot help but contribute something that is beautiful to our world. It is a gift that only you can share. That gift is the AUTHENTIC YOU! So as this step comes to an end, take the time to determine what it is you sincerely want in your life. Examine how you want your journey to feel. Find the things that help you feel more alive today! Become consciously connected to what you believe is the best version of you in this moment. Find the path that will lead you toward that goal and dream you'd like to create and each day commit to your purpose of doing the best you can. This is a process and the beginning of the formula. As you continue along with me in this book know that this step will give you the blueprint for your extraordinary life!

GET CONNECTED

It is extremely important for all of us to find and stay connected to the things that help bring out the beauty within us. We've all had those moments of magic where we feel how incredible life can be. The following questions are designed to help you become more aware while creating a conscious contact of what we already do and what we can do to help ourselves experience the magic and wonder of our lives each and everyday. Let's take some time now and reflect upon and answer the following questions.

1. Describe in detail an experience where you've felt the magic of your life – a time when you were just having a BLAST! What were you doing and why did it feel so good?

2. When was the last time you felt really good about yourself – the last time you did something that made you feel proud?

3. Describe an experience where you felt really STRESSED OUT! How did you react to that situation? How, if possible, could you have reacted better?

4. Describe an experience or a time where you felt peaceful and relaxed.

5. What do you do to relax?

6. What is your favorite physical activity?

7. What are some things you can do that you feel confident about, that you're good at? Describe the last time you did one of those things and how it felt inside to do it. We want details.

8. Who is your best friend, the person who knows you better than anyone else in the world? Why is this person considered the best?

9. Make a list of people in your life that you feel are healthy relationships, the people who help you feel good about you. Next to each persons name pick one word that best describes them.

10. Describe a time in your life when someone gave you a compliment that has stayed with you through the years. Who said it and what did they say? How did it make you feel to receive such a compliment?

11. Describe a time in your life where someone criticized you and it has stayed with you thru the years. What did they say and how did it make you feel?

12. Of the previous two questions, which do you hear more often within yourself and why?

13. When was the last time you laughed uncontrollably? A time where you laughed so hard you almost wet your pants (or maybe you did). Describe the whole story of what made you laugh so hard.

14. Do you have a religion? If so, which? Are you active in practicing or participating in your religious beliefs? How do they play a part

in your life? How do you deal with people who have different beliefs than you?

15. Have you ever experienced a moment that you would describe as spiritual? If so, describe the experience in detail.

16. Finally, describe your perfect day. From the moment you wake up until you go to bed at night. What would you do with your time? Who would you be with? What would you eat? See? Would you take a nap? Money is no object. You can do anything you want – in one day – what would it be?

In answering the previous questions it can help you discover on a deeper level "Who you are" which in turn can help you understand what it is you truly want. Everything else stems from there. Being able to define in your mind and your heart the life you want will begin the creation process. Everything around us began first as an idea…Think about that.

"Once begun halfway done." This was what my first running coach, Herb Rosen back in the 5th grade used to say to me. It was his way of motivating me to GET STARTED! One thing I have found in my quest to motivate others is how challenging it can be to just getting people started. It has also been a challenge for me. The major difference between those who succeed and those who struggle comes down to those who take action on their idea's, goals and dreams from those who don't. In the world of competitive running, a good start is crucial to success in any race. At the start of a race, people jostle for position. I find this very same thing happens in life. We seem to be constantly jostling for position in our families, careers and relationships. What does it take to get off to a "good" start?" How can we better position ourselves for success? I believe the answer comes from a deeper knowing and understanding of self. In order to come to a deeper understanding of where we may be going, we need to look to where we've been. Understanding and articulating the stories of your life can help you realize how and why you've come to where you are today. People throughout much of my life have asked me when I became a runner? Let me take you back to that very day.

"YOU HAVE A GIFT"

Ever since I was a little boy I was always very energetic and hyperactive. I would just love to run! Whenever my Mom brought me to the mall, the moment I saw the openness and limitless possibilities, I would just take-off. My mother would spend most of her time searching for me and the security guards knew me by name. I just couldn't contain myself and I never sat still. When I turned 7 years old my Dad signed me up for little league baseball. From the moment I was introduced to "America's past time" I just loved it! Baseball became everything to me. I collected the cards, I idolized the players and I just wanted to play all the time. My first 3 years in little league, I was named an all-star. I set the record for home runs, not because of how far I would hit the ball but rather because once I made any contact at all I just wouldn't stop running. I would get into run-downs between each base and eventually I'd end up at home because they simply couldn't catch me. (Nowadays advancing bases in such a way is no longer allowed) Springtime was my favorite time of year because that was baseball season. I was the pitcher, the shortstop and the center fielder! I could do it all. Baseball was my sport and I'd hoped that one day I'd be like my idol, Freddie Lynn, center fielder for the Boston Red Sox! Good old #19 was the first player to be named league MVP & Rookie of the year in the same year. My dream was to one day be just like him. That all changed when I was 10 years old.

It was the summer of 1977 and one of the first big transitions in the life of a kid was about to happen for me. I was getting ready to start Junior High School. Cass junior high in Darien, Illinois was different from all the other junior High's because you started in the 5th grade. Every other junior high in the county started in 6th grade but for whatever reason we began

22

in 5th. I remember I was excited to go to Cass because in Junior High they have organized school athletics. I could play sports for my school and I just thought that was the coolest thing. In the fall you had a choice of two different sports, Football & something called Cross Country. Seeing as how I didn't know what cross-country was I had my heart set on being a tailback for the Football team. The only drawback was that I was one of the smallest kids in my class but in Junior High they played flag football so I felt I had a fighting chance. I'd found out that tryouts would be at 3:30pm after school on the first day. I would be ready.

The first day had finally arrived and my Dad came into my room at 5am and woke me up saying, "Son, get your sweats on and your gym shoes and meet me in the garage in 5 minutes!" My first thought was, "Uh Oh, what did I do in the garage?" He had said it in such a way where you didn't question him you just did what you were told. So I rubbed my eyes, got out of bed and got my sweats on. A few minutes later I entered the garage where my Dad was already sitting in his car. I got in and we exited the garage without a word. I asked my Dad, "Where are we going?" I got no response at all. Eventually, I fell asleep because it was still dark outside seeing and 5:15 in the morning. A few minutes later my Dad in his ever so gentle way decided to wake me up my beeping the car horn as loudly as he could. I literally jumped out of my seat scared to death. My Dad said "Wake up son, were here. Now get out of the car and follow me." I immediately recognized where we were. We were at a local park and my Dad had quickly exited the car and was marching away. This park is a beautiful place with rolling hills and big beautiful trees. My Dad started up one of the hills and I lagged close behind. As I caught up to my Dad we had emerged at the top of one of the hills just as the morning sun was coming up. We both stopped for a moment and admired the beautiful sunrise. Then without a word, my Dad was moving again down the other side to the flat land. Once we reached a big open space my Dad stopped turned and said to me rather seriously, "Son, I brought you out here this morning because you and I are gonna have a race." I was confused as I looked up at him and simply responded, "What?" He repeated, "We're gonna have a race!" So I said quite naturally, "Why?" He got down on one knee looked me in the eyes and continued, "I understand that this afternoon is tryouts for fall sports at school and you are planning on going out for the football team. I've noticed something very special about you. I believe you have a gift. Now a gift is something very unique that not everybody has. Ever since you were a little guy you've always been the fastest kid around. Whether it's at the playground, the baseball field or in the mall, you've always been able to run like the wind. I don't know if you know this but I had the same ability and that's how I recognize it in you. That's why I brought you out here this morning. I want to test that gift. So you and I are gonna race once around the perimeter of this park. It's about a mile. We are going to head this way and make our way around counter clockwise until you reach that big oak tree about 200 yards behind us. Once you we get to that tree, we're gonna turn left and head right back to this spot. Where we are standing now will be the starting line and the finish line. If you are able to beat me then you should really consider trying out for the Cross Country team this afternoon instead of the football team." I looked at my Dad disappointed and said, "But Dad, I want to play football." The problem with football & me is that its not a natural fit. Remember, I was one of the smallest kids in the class and I believe my Dad was a little frightened that I'd get creamed on the football field. I also know that my Dad meant every word he was saying about this "Gift" he saw in me and I have to admit I was intrigued. "Son lets just have this race and see how good you actually are." You see my Dad knew I was very competitive. As far as I can remember I always had that competitive steak inside me. I always wanted to be the best. I looked my Dad square in his eyes and said, "Ok, lets do this!"

My Dad stood tall next to me and said, "On your marks, get set... GO!" My Dad jumped out to the lead and I remember thinking to just get right behind him and see if I could keep up. As we began to make our way around the park I noticed it felt pretty easy keeping up with him. At about the half way point I thought to myself, "I'm gonna pass him and take the lead, let's see if he can keep up with me." As I pulled alongside him to pass him, my Dad looked down at me and began running faster not allowing me to get by him. I surged again but he wouldn't let me by so I tucked back in behind him. As we came upon the 3/4mile mark my Dad started to run faster as I was getting tired. I began to fall behind, 5 yards, 10 yards, 15 yards behind when my Dad reached the Oak tree turned left and headed for the finish line. When I got to the Oak tree and turned left I remember a voice shouting in my head, "CATCH HIM!!!"

I remember, feeling that drive inside me! I remember deciding to fight thru the pain. I was gonna catch him! Something propelled me forward. It was like I had to catch him. Over the next 100 yards I could feel him coming back to me. I remember staring in the middle of his back and slowly reeling him in. With 100 yards left to go I had pulled even with him but I didn't even hesitate as I got beside him and began to take over the lead. But that wasn't going to fly with my Dad as he immediately ran faster and took back the lead! That made me mad and I ran even faster regaining the lead again but my Dad unrelentingly did the same. With about 20 yards to go I gave it all I had and pulled even with him. The two of us ran neck and neck down to the finish until at the last moment I lunged my body forward and beat my Dad by a step! I immediately fell to the ground gasping for air. My Dad stood over me, hands on his knees and said 5 words that would forever change my life: "SON, YOU ARE A RUNNER!"

That afternoon they had tryouts for football & cross-country and all day long I struggled with what to do. Football was something I had fun playing with my friends almost every Saturday at the park during the fall and I was good. I was good because I was faster then everybody else but in reality I was one of the smallest kids in my grade. It was my speed that made me special. It was my endurance that made me formidable. I could just outlast everyone. My energy seemed limitless. All throughout that day I kept hearing my Dads words echoing within me, "Son, you are a runner." So when 3:30pm rolled around I found myself reporting to Mr. Rosen's classroom, the head Cross Country coach. Once signed in, all the runners made there way behind the school to the adjacent fields. Mr. Rosen lined us up and told us we'd be running twice around the perimeter of the field. The distance was about a mile. My second mile race in the same day, but this time instead of racing my Dad I was racing against kids from all grades, 5th thru 8th. "OKAY...RUNNERS SET..." Off went the starters pistol and about 150 kids bolted off the starting line. We had one kid in our school that was known as the best. He was an 8th grader and his name was Sammie Ramont. He was kind of a legend in the neighborhood since he finished 8th in the county championships as a 7th grader. He went right to the lead and just as I did that morning with my Dad, I got right behind him. The first 1/2 mile was no big deal as I stayed right on Sammie's tail, exactly how it was with my Dad. I remember Sammie kept looking back to see who this little kid was running with him. The two of us had pulled away from everyone else as we completed the first lap. We were easily about 100 yards ahead of the rest of the pack. As we passed by Mr. Rosen at the 1/2 way mark I remember the smile he had on his face as he watched in disbelief. I even remember him calling out to the head football Coach who would eventually be my first track Coach Mr. Curran, saying, "Hey Charlie, you seeing this?" Mr. Curran replied, "Who is that kid?" That moment, I felt this rush of pride roll thru me. My Dad was right. I had a gift. I could run! As we got 1/2 way around the final lap, Sammie started pushing the pace. I tried valiantly to keep up with him but he began to pull away. By the time we reached the finish, Sammie crossed the line first and I came in about 7 seconds behind him in second. Third place came thru about 20 seconds behind me. As I stood at the finish line with hands on my knees trying to catch my breath, Mr. Rosen put his hand on my back and said, "Holy cow kid, you can run!"

What I had realized on that very first day of Junior High was that I really liked the attention that came from being special. I liked how the kids and the adults looked at me that day. I loved feeling as though I was really good at something. It played right into a natural competitiveness that I had. I went on to finish 12th place in the county championships my 5th grade year. I finished 3rd my 6th grade year and I was the County Champion my 7th & 8th grade years. It wasn't so much the running that I liked, that just came natural. It was the winning that I liked. It was the attention that I liked. It was the looks I'd get from my competitors when I stepped to the starting line. It was the confidence I felt after a race I'd just won as I walked off the course. That became a very important state of mind for me. A feeling that would stay with me and drive so many of my behaviors as I grew up. That feeling of being the best actually became a need in me. It helped me feel as though I was worthy. It's what gave me my self-esteem. It also became one of the heaviest burdens I would carry throughout my life for the joy came from the winning and not the sport itself. If I wasn't the best, then who was I?

This drive and ultra competitiveness found its way into almost every area of my life. Whatever the game, whatever the competition, I had to win. Now contrast that with an underlying deep seeded fear of abandonment. I was not easy to get along with all the time because I had to be "better" than you. But I was also a people pleaser and wanted every one around me to be happy and harmonious. These two sides of who I am we're in constant conflict for most of my life. It took me a long time to discover this about me. I was living a "reactionary" life not truly understanding or making the connection as to what this was creating in my world. So when I got married and we'd fight or argue or have any stress at all she would retreat either emotionally or physically, this would kick in my abandonment issue and I would work to fix it. Yet one of the hardest things for me when we'd have conflict would be to back down or walk away because of my competitiveness and my need to be right. Thus, I was adding more stress to the situation or argument and actually pushing her to the point where she would leave. It was a vicious cycle in our marriage that actually began early in our courtship. Sometimes in my mind, the things that would set her off would be ridiculous or trivial yet it would be made into a big thing because I believe we were both stuck in this pattern, this way of being and relating to each other that it almost became like oxygen to us. In other words, it was something that we needed. It was our "normal" it was our comfort zone. It's what we both knew. Its amazing to me now how long we went on like that and the ironic thing is with my need to be righteous I was married to someone who in her estimation was never wrong and who never apologized. It was the "perfect storm" of issues coming together to create quite a dysfunctional relationship. But after awhile it was all we knew...and it was very hard.

I'm getting a bit ahead of myself but an examination of the roots can tell you volumes about the life itself. That is why I find it imperative to live an examined life to better understand how to move forward. This is all part of what it means when I say "getting off to a good start." If you want or rather need to change something in your life in order to move forward, the first key is enlightenment and understanding what the issue might be. Now please don't misunderstand me, I do not believe that our past equals our future. I do however believe that it has something to do with who we are today and how we think and what we believe. Our identity has been formulated based on the past and I believe we live our lives consciously or unconsciously to be congruent with the identity we have cultivated for ourselves. The sad reality is that most people are not even fully aware of what that identity is. How do we become aware?

Our decisions and actions flow from our identity and in this way our values help to define us. Our exploration and discovery of our identity is therefore a discovery of self. Ask yourself how you discover who other people are? When meeting someone we typically exchange our names and then inevitably the question that follows is, "What do you do?" What are people really asking when they inquire about what you do? They are asking about your job, profession or vocation for sure but the fact that this question comes out so quickly indicates how highly we rate work in our culture and how closely we identify ourselves with what work we do. When people ask what you do they are in essence trying to discover who you are. They are hoping for an answer that will help them quickly get to know you. So imagine someone is asking you that question but it has nothing to do with your occupation. Here is how I'd answer.

"So Eddie, what do you do?"

"Well I guess I do many things. I play with and take care of my Children. I hang out with and talk to my wife. I spend time with my family. I teach. I learn. I listen. I dance. I laugh. I love music. I play music. I am competitive. I care what others think and feel about me. I try to make others laugh. I go to the movies. I write. I exercise. I entertain. I read. I take care of others. I ask questions. I seek answers. I argue. I love a good party. I drink tea. I meditate. I speak. I motivate. I empower. I inspire."

None of these things need to be necessarily good or bad but they do need to be what you devote time to. The people and things we love in our lives are the things we give our TIME. For everything we give time to and prioritize, we need to ask "WHY" we care about it? In doing so we can understand the core of our thinking. We need to be aware of the things around which we construct our lives. We need to be certain of the foundation we are building upon. Is my life in congruency with how I see myself? Finally, do I understand who I truly am? What is the essence of me? These are all key questions we need answers for as we construct WHAT we want in our lives and WHY.

THIS IS THE FIRST STEP TO THE FORMULA AND THE LAUNCHING POINT. DETERMINE WHAT YOU WANT & WHY. WHEN YOU'VE DONE THIS YOU ARE ON YOUR WAY!!!

Before we move on to the 2nd step in the formula I want to share with you some empowering quotes. The first 25 are quotes I came up with and have shared with my audiences over the years. The next 25 are from some of my heroes.

EDDIE'S QUOTES:

1. There is greatness within you!

2. The deepest most profound type of poverty is poverty of the soul.

3. The power in visualizing what you want to create in your life helps you believe that it's possible and when you believe something is possible it motivates you in the NOW to do something about it.

4. Visualization is not just about your future it is about changing the present path you are on leading you toward your future.

5. Imagination is one of the most powerful tools we possess in building the life we want.

6. You are so much more than your doubts, fears and insecurities.

7. It doesn't matter what others say, it's what we hear that counts.

8. My truth, my voice, my authentic self is what matters most.

9. It is the pain and suffering in my life that has created in me the qualities I am most proud of.

10. It is not the destination that is most important, it is the journey on the way to our destination.

11. What you believe about you is what's motivating most of what you do in your life. The dilemma we face is that most of our beliefs are unconscious to us.

12. As soon as I think I know it all, I've just decided to stop growing as a person.

13. The most important aspect in listening is not done with your ears, it's done with your eyes & your heart.

14. Listening is a proactive endeavor. If we are passive listeners we really are "Not Hearing" what others are trying to say to us.

15. In every race I've run, whether I was 1st place or last, PAIN always had a say in the outcome. I believe the same is true in life. Accept it.

16. In my view, the most important relationship in your life is the one you have with YOU!

17. The key to living my best life comes down to forgiveness. Forgiving those who have harmed us starting first and foremost with ourselves.

18. Our story can inform us as to "who" we are today and help us more deeply understand why we do the things we do. As our story continues, we must try to learn from our past and then let go in order to fully immerse ourselves in the present.

19. Being fully present to another is one of the greatest gifts you can give.

20. At times I do worry about what others think, but I have learned to worry more about what I think.

21. To be outer-focused means to give up the power over what we may discover to be our authentic selves.

22. The deepest experience of happiness and joy I have had in my life has not come from what I get, it comes from what I give.

23. I like to speak on my experience of life for it is really the only topic in which I have true creditability.

24. Sometimes we get so focused on what we cannot control when maybe it's time to focus on what we can.

25. My focus, my perspective of me in this world plays a huge role in my actions and decisions and how I experience this thing we call life.

FAMOUS QUOTES:

1. Ben Franklin: "An investment in knowledge pays the best interest"

2. Gandhi: "We must become the change we want to see in the world"

3. Winston Churchill: "Success is not final and failure is not fatal. It is the courage to continue that counts."

4. Dr. Martin Luther King, Jr.: "Love is the only force capable of turning an enemy to a friend."

5. Walt Disney: "If you can dream it you can do it"

6. Abraham Lincoln: "The best thing about the future is that it comes only one day at a time"

7. Vince Lombardi: "The quality of a persons life is in direct proportion to their commitment to excellence, regardless of their chosen field of endeavor"

8. Eleanor Roosevelt: "No one can make you feel inferior without your consent"

9. Helen Keller: "The best and most beautiful things in life cannot be seen, not touched, but are felt in the heart"

10. Pope John Paul II: "The worst prison would be a closed heart"

11. George Patton: "If a man does his best, what else is there?"

12. Booker T. Washington: "There are two ways of exerting ones strength; one is pushing down, the other is pulling up"

13. Albert Schweitzer: "Success is not the key to happiness. Happiness is the key to success. If you love what you are doing, you will be successful"

14. Harry S. Truman: "It is amazing what you can accomplish if you do not care who gets the credit"

15. Mother Teresa: "In this life we cannot always do great things, but we can do small things with great love."

16. Anonymous: "In life you'll meet two types of people, ones that build you up and ones that tear you down but in the end you'll thank them both"

17. William James: "The greatest weapon against stress is our ability to choose one thought over another"

18. Ralph Waldo Emerson: "To be yourself in a world that is constantly trying to make you something else is the greatest accomplishment"

19. Maya Angelou: "There is no greater agony than bearing the untold story inside of you"

20. Albert Einstein: "Great spirits have always encountered violent opposition from mediocre minds"

21. Muhammad Ali: "I am the greatest! I said that before I knew I was"

22. Michael Jordan: I've missed over 9000 shots in my career. I've lost almost 300 games. 26 times I've been trusted to take the game winning shot and missed. I've failed over and over and over again in my life and that is why I succeed."

23. John Lennon: "Life is what happens to you while you're busy making other plans"

24. Buddha: "The mind is everything. What you think you become"

25. Mark Twain: "Twenty years from now you will be more disappointed by the things that you didn't do, so throw off the bow lines, sail away from safe harbor, catch the trade winds in your sails. Explore, Dream, Discover."

STEP #2:

BELIEVE

Transformation begins with awareness. If we want to grow and strive to be our better self then we need to be mindful of how we see ourselves in the present. There are many things affecting our perspective. The more we become aware of the factors that influence perspective the more we able to understand the direction of our lives. We are conditioned creatures and our "story" plays a major role in how we perceive ourselves. This present perspective is directly affecting the choices we make and the future we are creating. Breaking thru the conditioning of our lives is not an easy task. First you need recognition. Recognition and awareness can help us break through the disillusionment that can often take place. Moving beyond the cultural conditioning of our everyday existence can be liberating. Becoming fully aware is key. Awareness has no other quality other than awareness. It is not a culture, it doesn't belong to any religion and it's not male or female. Awareness is natural and it is here and now. It helps us to awaken and pay attention in a deeper way. In the world of athletics it's known as "Being in the Zone." When we access this state of mind, we see things we may not otherwise see. We understand things in a more meaningful way. We are better able to guide ourselves to where we'd like to be. Being "self aware" is the one thing that can truly help expand our lives and help us grow. Each one of us must first lead ourselves toward the life we desire.

Our state of "well-being" comes down to our mind and its awareness. Like an athlete trains his or her body to be fit, our minds need training too. Mind training is grounded in the idea and understanding that two opposite mental factors cannot happen at the same time. You can go from Love to Hate but you cannot experience both at the same time towards the same object or the same person. Thus, a natural cure to the emotions that are destructive to our inner life is the fact that it cannot last or take up residence in our awareness unless we allow it. All emotions are fleeting and the only way it can linger is because of the focus and awareness we choose to give it. Each time our minds go to the emotions that cause us pain it reinforces that emotions power. It becomes a self-perpetuating process that if we're not aware of becomes our life's experience.

To begin a new process and awareness, instead of looking outward we need to look inward. We need to look into the depth of who we are. On the surface of our minds as a negative thought and emotion arises we do not need to attach ourselves to that thought by giving it total focus. For example, a thought of what someone did to you in your past that makes you feel anger. If we dwell on the thought and pay mind to it then it will create the emotion of anger. Next the body quickly follows suit with tension and stress thus creating the physical experience of that anger. We are now not just experiencing anger we ARE angry. What if, as the initial thought arises of what that person did that caused us anger we choose not to give it our awareness? What happens then? Well, the thought will pass like the clouds passing overhead in the sky and our awareness might now be on the sun that was behind the clouds giving us warmth. Now we are in a whole new experience. This training of the mind is not easy just as running a sub four-minute mile wasn't easy. It is a process. The body responds to consistent training. Our minds work much in the same way. It took us years to develop the way in which our minds work so it will take time to experience a new way. In the training itself, in the practice, we can experience the awareness of something new, something positive. This positivity along the journey will help us continue down that path. This mind transformation takes daily practice. This is why so many people are discovering meditation. Meditation is mind & body transformation.

In recent years scientists and researchers have made great strides in the area of brain plasticity. It used to be believed that by the time you reach adulthood that your brain was about as developed as it could get. It was believed that any changes in the brain once we hit adulthood are insignificant if there is any change at all. We now know this simply isn't true. The brain has incredible plasticity meaning its potential to change and adapt at any stage of life is not only possible it is rather quite probable. In order for such changes to take place will require significant practice. The training of the mind needs to be a daily, ongoing and consistent endeavor. A few years back a comprehensive study was done on Buddhist monks from various parts of the world. They were considered experts in the practice of meditation. They placed them in an MRI for 3 1/2 hours as they meditated to observe the activity of the brain. What they found was that they were able to significantly increase the activity in the left side of the pre frontal cortex. In fact, in some cases the activity in this part of the brain was off the charts! Why is this significant? This was significant because that is the side where we experience and feel compassion, love and happiness. This showed the researchers that mind training not only works but that it also matters. What I believe to be most significant about this is when we practice mind training and we work on meditation, it increases our experience of love & compassion, which in turn inspires us to want to share that love & compassion. Thus, it is not only good for us it is good for the world.

THE POWER OF ONE'S VISION

Did you know that when we experience something and when we visualize the same thing we actually activate the same brain circuits? Therefore, the

Brain does not know the difference between a real "experience" from the same visualized or imagined one. The reason for this is due to an area in the brain known as **THE RETICULAR ACTIVATING SYSTEM**. This is a part of the Brain that acts as a filter to the conscious mind. It selects what will be noticed and given attention to by the conscious mind. By utilizing visualization you can purposefully begin to notice the steps needed to create and enhance the actual experience. A Harvard study found that participants who visualized only in their mind a simple 5 finger Piano sequence for 2 hours a day for 5 consecutive days created the same pathways and changes within the brain as those participants who actually physically did the process. The practice of visualization can literally rewire our brain and create epigenetic changes within our bodies. This is why IMAGINATION is such an important key to creation.

MY INTRODUCTION TO THE POWER OF IMAGAINATION

When I was 4 years old, the seeds of imagination and visualization and the power they can have on our lives were planted in me during the very first movie going experience I'd ever had. The year was 1971 and it was my 4th birthday, one of my favorite people ever, my Aunt Peggy was taking me to a movie to celebrate. I was so excited because I had never been to a movie before. I will never forget that day. In fact, when I reminisce and visualize that day its like I'm reliving it. I remember it was raining and we had to run from the car into the theater so as not to get soaked. When we entered the doors of the theatre it was like stepping into some new & amazing world filled with lavish colors and incredible smells! The freshly made popcorn filling my nostrils was a thrill and I knew I was in some magical place. When we walked into the theatre I was blown away by the size of the screen. I had never seen anything so big! Then we found some seats in the middle and we hunkered down with popcorn & raisinets. We had gotten there early to insure good seats. I was so little that my feet barely reached the end of the seat I was sitting on. As the place filled up my heart just raced. The theater was packed! Then the lights went out and I heard the whirring sound of the projector as the screen lit up and it read: "WILLIE WONKA AND THE CHOCOLATE FACTORY"

I was having the time of my life being whisked away to this amazing World of Willie Wonka! The scene I will never forget that had a huge impact on me was when during the tour of the factory they entered this one unforgettable room. It began with them walking in a hallway where they seemed to get bigger or the hallway was shrinking, you couldn't really tell. He then opens this huge door as he said, "Ladies and Gentlemen, Boys and Girls...THE CHOCOLATE ROOM." As the door opens we see this magnificent room that looks like a rainbow forest filled with brilliant colors and scrumptious looking candies, whipped cream, gummie bears, lollipops and of course a chocolate river filled by a chocolate waterfall! In other words, it looked like a child's heaven. What made this room so unique is that everything within it was edible. You could eat anything and everything that was there!!! Before Willie Wonka allows them to go explore and feast he tells them to hold their breath, make a wish and count to three. Then he sang a song that most of us who have seen this Movie will never forget about the power of pure imagination!

What Willie Wonka was telling those kids in that moment is that everything you've seen in this factory and everything you'll see in this amazing Chocolate Room began within his imagination. Every time I hear this song or watch this scene I am transported back to what I was feeling on that day. It was a feeling I had never experienced before. I didn't know what I was feeling I just knew that it felt amazing! I couldn't articulate what I was experiencing I was so young. Now I am able to understand what it was I was feeling, I was INSPIRED!!!

This scene illustrates the power of our imagination. Willie Wonka challenges to utilize that power to begin the creation process.

This is a perfect way to describe the importance of the second step in the formula: BELIEVE! When we are able to visualize or imagine what it is we want to do, our conscious mind begins to believe that the destination we imagine is now possible for us. Why is this so important? Because that belief will fuel the actions and choices that need to happen in the present to begin the creation of it.

THE BEST WAY TO PREDICT YOUR FUTURE IS TO CREATE YOUR FUTURE!

By consciously visualizing our future it can change our present. Our beliefs drive so much of what we do and what we don't do. In order to set ourselves up for living the better versions of who we can be we MUST start with the belief that we can create the life of our dreams. For what it comes down to is the understanding that the power lies in the choices and actions we take in the present moment. This is where our lives are happening. Therefore, we must find the motivation and the inspiration to create. Visualize where it is you want to be and what you want to do and how you want to feel and then take action. One important thing to mention is that the primary focus of our lives needs to be on the present. It is the journey where we experience the fullness of our lives. Believing in the possibility of what your life can be will ultimately enhance and elevate your life experience. This is the very thing that will take your life from ordinary to extraordinary!

WHEN IT HIT HOME

I have a very powerful experience with my Dad and how he taught me to be a forward thinker and how having "vision" can change the direction of your life. I had just finished freshmen year in high school with straight "C's" and it was mid summer as I lay on the couch watching the Cubs lose again. Earlier that day I had been fired from my 4th job in a month. I should have been out running and putting in my summer miles but instead I was being lazy. That first year in High School I became the 2nd best distance runner in the school as a freshman. I also garnered a reputation and a nickname: "SLACKMAN." My coach as well as my teammates called me this because I was by far the laziest kid on the team. To say I was not a hard worker would be an understatement. My Dad walked in and was visibly upset to see me sitting there. He called me into his bedroom and it felt like I was meeting with the Godfather! I was nervous because my Father had a propensity for screaming at you when you weren't living up to his expectations. But on this day he wasn't yelling at me instead he asked me a question. "Son, do you remember that job I had in corporate America?" I nodded yes while still bracing for his wrath. He continued, "Do you remember me talking about my old boss who was one of my heroes?" Again I nodded in the affirmative and again he continued. "I'd like to tell you how my old boss created the company that I used to work for. It is a story about something that I believe is missing in your life and it is something you need to hear." I was intrigued and relieved because he wasn't yelling. My Father began the story:

"My old bosses name was Ray and he used to be a travelling sales-man. Ray had been selling paper goods for quite sometime and was quite good at it however he was bored. One day he saw a new product come on the market called, "The Multi Mixer." This was a revolutionary new Milk Shake Machine. Ray thought it was fabulous and he wanted to sell it! The problem though was that this would be an expensive move. Ray had to mortgage his home and spend his entire life savings to pay for the rights to become the Midwest Distributor of The Multi Mixer. Ray was now licensed to sell this machine. He thought this could be the product that would help him reach his dream of becoming a millionaire!

This new venture did not begin well. Ray was having tremendous difficulty selling this machine. He was calling ice cream parlors, restaurants and anywhere else he could think that served milk shakes. Six months in, Ray was worried he was going to go bankrupt because he couldn't generate any interest in the Multi Mixer. Then one day, Ray got a call from a restaurant in San Bernardino, California. To Ray's great surprise they ordered 8 Multi Mixers! That was such a big order that Ray thought it was a mistake so he called the restaurant to confirm. When the order was confirmed Ray told the owners of the restaurant that he would deliver them personally from Chicago where he lived. He told them to give him about a week to make the journey. So Ray packed his trunk and headed west. About 5 days later Ray pulled into the parking lot of the address he was given and was immediately concerned because it was just a small little place sitting atop a hill. He thought to himself, There's no way this little place wants 8 Multi Mixers! Ray ventured inside the restaurant and asked to speak to the owners. Two men walked up, introduced themselves and were delighted to see Ray and more importantly get their hands on those Multi Mixers. Ray inquired, "Are you sure you will need 8 of these machines?" They replied an enthusiastic, "Yes, we will need all 8." So Ray brought them in, set them up on the counter and showed them how they worked. Ray then said he'd be willing to hang around that day and help out until they were comfortable with the machines. They were thrilled with the level of service Ray was willing to offer. So quickly showed them how to operate them then he stepped back out of the way as they prepared to open their doors.

It didn't take long for Ray to see that they most certainly would need all 8 of the Multi Mixers because business was booming! They had a constant stream of customers coming thru those doors throughout the day and just about everybody was ordering a milk shake with their meal. Ray was hustling about helping out while being incredibly impressed with the operation they had going on there. Half way thru that day Ray had a vision. In his mind, in his imagination Ray was able to visualize this little restaurant all over America! He could see it! He truly believed this little place could flourish anywhere and everywhere. This completely thrilled Ray and with this enthusiasm he came up with an idea.

Ray waited patiently until the last customer made their way to the door and the business day was done to share his idea. He went up to the two owners who also happened to be brothers and he said,

"Gentlemen, I'd like to make you an offer. I will give you 1 million dollars if you give me the ownership rights to this restaurant!"

Needless to say this offer came as a shock to these brothers for this was 1954 and a million dollars was an incredible amount of money back then. They immediately became skeptical and responded with, "why do you want to do this?" Undaunted, Ray responded,

"Because I love what you have created here and I'd like to build one just like it back in Chicago where I'm from and maybe a few other places. In order to do this, the way I would like I would need to own it. One million dollars is my offer."

The two brothers looked at one another, smiled and extended their hands to shake on the deal and as they did responded with a resounding, "For One Million dollars, you've got a deal!"

There was one major problem; Ray did not have a million dollars. He explained to them that he would need to head back to Chicago and get the investors he'd need to make this happen. The two brothers wanted to know how long that would take and Ray was not sure. Feeling deflated the two brothers proclaimed that this would not work. They explained how they'd tried something similar in the past and it just didn't work. Ray was persistent though and eventually he convinced them to let him try. Ray then did as he promised, he went back to Chicago and found the investors and raised the capitol he needed. He headed back to San Bernardino ready to finalize this deal. He brought with him a binding contract and a cashier's check with the money they had thought would be impossible to get. He triumphantly walked through the doors and told the brothers,

"I have your money! Are you ready to do this deal?"

The two brothers read the contract and felt everything was in order. They did have one question for Ray.

"Before we sign this we would like to know what you plan to call this place?"

Ray replied,

"I'm glad you asked me that. I've been thinking long and hard about that and I would like to keep the name you guys gave it, it's a great name, with one exception. I'd like to take the word "Brothers" off of the end of it."

The two brothers were happy that what they created would carry on with their name. They signed the contract and the restaurant known as "McDonalds" was born.

When my dad finished he looked at me and said,

"Now Son, do you know why I told you this story?"

I replied,

"Nope."

My Dad continued, "Son I told you this story because I wanted you to understand the power that vision can play in a persons life. Understand that I'm not talking about the vision from your eyes, I'm talking about the vision from your heart. I'm talking about your dreams, your goals your aspirations. I never hear you talk about your future. I never hear you talk about your dreams. You are one of the best runners your High School has seen in a generation yet you've earned a reputation and a nickname that every time I hear it, it embarrasses me and you think is funny. "Slackman" simply means you're lazy! You ended the year with straight C's when you and I both know you are smarter than that. You're just not working hard enough! And you just got fired from your 5th job this summer! Son, where do you think all these decisions you're making are leading you? If you keep this up your life is going to be a major struggle for you'll be heading nowhere. You need to at some point stop just thinking about where you are but rather where you'd like to be! When you get clear on where it is you want to go then you're able to understand more deeply what it is you need to do to get there. Ray Kroc was just a guy trying to sell milk shake machines until he happened to venture into McDonald Brothers restaurant. While there he was able to see the potential of what that place could become. His vision for the future is what inspired him. The McDonald brothers could only see what they had and thus that's as far as they got! Son, you can be many things in this world. What does your heart tell you and what do you believe you are capable of? I can see great things for you but what matters most is what you can see for yourself."

I will never forget that day. My Fathers words resonate with me today and always. On that day I became a "forward thinker." Thinking beyond my present to where I hope to be. This way of living fuels our drive and gives us hope. That is why in every company or organization that I consult, one of the first things that must be created is a "Shared Vision." The power of belief is an astounding thing. It is the very thing that will begin to lift us up to a new realm of achievement so before we embark on the actual work to accomplish our goals we must have a clear vision on what we want to do and what we believe we can do. That's the beauty of the power of visualization for it fuels our belief, which in turn fuels our actions, our choices and our behavior.

During my live presentations and seminars sometimes I will have a volunteer come on stage to illustrate the power of visualization and what it can do for us. I will lay down some tape down horizontally on the stage and have them stand behind it. I then explain how I want them to do a broad jump (where you bend your knees and leap out and in the air) as far as they can and when they land I want them to land flat footed for I will mark how far they were able to go based on where their heels end up. I then stand out of the way and let them do their thing. When they land, I place tape directly behind their heels. I then have them sit down right in front of the leap they just made. I have them look closely at the distance they just covered. I want them to see what they had accomplished. Then I have them close their eyes and I tell them that they are going to jump again but before they do I'd like them to visualize it first. I want them to see it all happen in their minds before they actually do it. The key difference, I want them to visualize them jumping further then they did the first time. At that moment I put on the song, "EYE OF THE TIGER." This inevitably gets a laugh from the crowd and a smile from my volunteer. I want the music to spur them on to not only see the future but to get ready to create it! I then ask my volunteer, "Tell me when you can see it!" Once they say they can see it, I tell them to open their eyes and get back behind that line and make it happen. Before they make their 2nd leap I get the audience to cheer them on as loud as they can. The room is now electric and you can practically see the adrenalin flowing through the veins of our volunteer! Then they jump, and in every single case, my volunteer has gone further then they did the first time!

I believe with all my heart the reason the volunteer goes further the 2nd time is because they first visualized it in their minds and thus they believed it could be done. This power is extraordinary! In all the things I have learned as a world-class athlete and as a Peak Performance Speaker, Consultant & Author is that what one believes about oneself will be the precursor in what actually happens in their lives. The key is becoming aware of what those beliefs are.

So where do our beliefs come from? Could it be that our journey thus far and the people who have played a significant role in that journey actually have a hand in creating our beliefs? Without a doubt I believe the answer is YES! Why is a deeper understanding of our beliefs so vital? Our beliefs have played a huge role in the creation of our identity. Our identity plays a massive role in how we choose both consciously and more importantly unconsciously to live our lives. Another important point I'd like to make is the power of those who believe in us. Before my volunteer jumps for a second time I have the audience cheer them on with great enthusiasm. The reason for this, I want my volunteer to feel the power of support and the belief that others have for them. This is such a huge part of our ultimate success. We all need people in our corner who want to see us succeed. It's amazing how often I have found the opposite in our society. Many times it feels as though others like to see us fail. When we surround ourselves with toxic people who would rather see us fail, then we are in trouble. Who we call our friends, our inner circle, will have an ultimate say in our experience of life. It is so crucial that we surround ourselves with those who choose to believe in us. I heard it once said that we are the average of the 5 people we spend the most time with. Think for a moment and discover whether or not those 5 people in your life sincerely believe in you?

Mindfulness

One particular method I found in my search that can truly help when it comes to what I can control which could improve the quality of my life is "Mindfulness." This has become a hot topic as of late since we have become so "wired in" to technology in our lives. Because of all the gadgets we now align ourselves with, we have become more distracted than ever. I came upon this at a time that I was seeking distraction to help me cope or rather avoid coping with the problems of my marriage. Many experts actually believe that we can become addicted to distraction. Some of us build our lives around this very notion for it has become one of the main coping mechanisms we have. We become so set in our ways and habitually conditioned creatures that sometimes we may think that change is impossible. Oh sure, circumstances surrounding our lives can change but can we? It was once believed by the scientific community that our neural pathways are set during childhood and adolescence. This is no longer a widely held belief for scientists are learning more and more that our brains actually have the ability to adapt and rewire. Thru the use of brain scans, we are seeing that our brains can change through experiences and use. This phenomenon, known as Neuroplasticity, suggests there are concrete and provable benefits to exercising the brain. This is why living a more present or mindful life is gaining momentum in a vast and rapidly moving world of distraction.

Researchers have found that multitasking leads to lower overall productivity. People who are constantly moving from one task to the next are not as mindful as they can be in what they are doing and thus they make more mistakes which inevitably cuts down on efficiency and productivity. In his book, "thoughts become Things" author Mike Dooley suggests that

"We become aware of what we are thinking and simply do not allow ourselves to focus any longer on the thoughts that do not serve us well."

As I researched this more deeply I recognized the theory that since our thoughts are real things in our lives they are able to be the basis of our actions, choices and behaviors. So many thoughts come in and out of our mind yet we can choose certain thoughts as well. Whatever thoughts you choose manifest themselves in real ways in your life. When we choose thoughts in our lives it is an immutable law that they are now part of our lives and will in someway begin to affect what happens next. This understanding is revelatory and I find it to be helpful and true. My only issue is that I don't want to become robotic in the control of my thoughts and actions. As Joseph Campbell used to say, be sure to make room for the soul. Being more mindful can certainly begin to make an immediate difference while being quite powerful to utilize in life.

Researchers and scientists say that in any given day, human beings think upwards to about 50,000 thoughts so obviously we don't give our full mindfulness to all of them. The question then becomes, which thoughts do you choose to give your undivided attention and allegiance too? The more you think about a certain thing, the more you focus on it and the more you perpetuate it's existence in your future. So I guess we need to take a moment and think about what we think about. For being mindful and understanding how our thoughts manifest themselves in our lives can help us create more positive control over our well being. Scientists have been able to prove that mindfulness and meditation can lower cortisol levels and blood pressure, increase immune response and help us ward off potential sickness. This is why I have fully adopted this mindfulness idea in the many facets of my life. I've experienced mindfulness before but just hadn't realized it. We all have. When we wake up to this fact and become consciously aware that we can be more present then we will. This is profound because again it is something we CAN control. What I like most about is the realization that I can begin RIGHT NOW to make my experience of life so much better! It is amazing what we can do if we are aware, attentive and proactive.

One great endeavor that I find and experience in my work that so many of us are seeking is Happiness. No matter what ones goals or dreams seem to be the actual experience or manifestation of the goal is finding oneself in a state of fulfillment and happiness. That feeling of being happy seems to over shadow all other hopes or desires for most of us. People are desperately trying to find a road map to their own happiness. Because of this, there has become quite a study of happiness lately.

In the past, experts and researchers would look into why depression happens and how if affects our lives. No one was really looking into the root causes of happiness. As in anything, to be happy one must understand how happiness comes to be and how it manifests in one's life. Researchers have discovered that some of it is out of our control. About 50% of what makes us happy is built into our genetic code. We all know people who just seem more naturally happy than others. I don't happen to be one of them although I'd consider myself a fairly happy person. I am however intrigued by those who just seem intrinsically happy. That's probably why I am married again. Well, not probably why, it's exactly why! My wife Diane is one of the happiest people I have ever met. My nickname for her is "Sunshine." I call her this because it's how I feel when I am in her presence: Warm & Content. From the moment we first spoke on the phone, to the moment we first met to every single day I am in her presence, she just projects such warmth and happiness. I truly do become happier in her presence. So I guess that sometimes happiness is contagious and can literally rub off from one to another. Who we choose to surround ourselves with can truly make a difference in our experience of life. Think about it, we've all been around negative, complaining people and their mood and demeanor literally do have an affect on us. They can bring us down and suck all the life out of the room. Their negativity becomes the experience and thus we suffer. But enthusiastic, passionate, optimistic, happy people can breathe life back into us!

The actual experience of happiness within our brains is the release of a chemical called Dopamine. Through what's known as a neurotransmitter, dopamine gets released from the brain throughout the body thus creating the euphoric feeling of being happy. Research shows that one great way to have this happen more often is thru physical exertion. Exercise is a great way to release dopamine into the system, but actually finding and exploring new ways to have physical exertion or exercise works even better. Breaking routines and trying something in a new way is a great start. For example, you know I love to run. Running is my preferable form of exercise. These days most of my running is done on a treadmill at my local health club. However, when I take the time to go out to the forest preserve and run on the trails, that is when I've experienced some of my happiest moments. There is something about nature and trails where you have to fully focus and be present to each step so as not to turn an ankle. Because of this intense focus I have had moments of pure bliss. Part of that bliss is being experienced because I am completely immersed in the moment. It is creating what's known as the "runners high" that I'm sure you've heard about. This "high" is nothing more than dopamine flooding my system. To know that there are certain things I can do to help create this experience is very enlightening and empowering!

Some of the greatest performers have understood the power behind the art of visualization. Wayne Gretzky was once asked what made him such an amazing hockey player? He replied, "It has to be my vision out there on the ice. I don't skate to where the puck is, I skate to where it's going." This is so telling as to why he is considered the greatest hockey player ever. He is just one of many Peak Performers who understand the power of visualization. Let me share another great example.

One very special day I met THE G.O.A.T. (Greatest Of All Time) in the sport of basketball and I had the opportunity to ask him a question. I was embarking on training for the Olympic trials and I was struggling. This was a time of transition in my life and for many those times can be difficult. I had just graduated from college a few months earlier and s had lost my support network and my usual routine. I found myself not putting forth the effort it would take to realize my goal of making the trials and hopefully the Olympic team. I was depressed and not really knowing what to do next. Then one amazing day I found myself face to face with Michael Jordan in a hotel convention center. I decided to use that opportunity to seek out some answers from one of the greatest competitors in the history of sports. I took a deep breath, walked over to him, mustered up the courage and said,

"Excuse me, Mr. Jordan?"

Immediately he put me at ease as he turned and with a sheepish smile said,

"Hey, call me Michael."

I proudly put my hand out and way to excitedly exclaimed,

"Okay Michael, How Ya doin?" Without hesitation he shook my hand. I immediately followed up with,

"Would you mind if I ask you a question?"

With the smile still on his face he said,

"Go right ahead."

So I asked,

"You're a big hero of mine and without a doubt one of the greatest competitors of all time. I really admire the way you play the game. You rarely seem to have a bad night and your performance is always excellent. My question to you is how do you do it? What helps you make this happen?"

Michael Jordan then stepped back and folded his arms and looked down at his feet. He was quiet for a few moments, which I really appreciated because he was actually thinking about my question and searching for an answer. He then responded with this:

"I'll tell you one thing that's always seemed to help. I think about what it is that I want to do. When I get a clear picture in my mind, when I can actually see it happening and when it feels right in my heart it's really helped me make it happen in my life."

When he finished I shook his hand and told him thank you and what an honor it was to meet him. I knew what he was talking about. He was talking about the power of visualization. I had utilized this technique in my life as a competitive runner but I had yet to realize its potential in other areas of life. Michael was a master at this and I'll never forget one particular time he displayed it and created the outcome he desired.

The year was 1997 and the Chicago Bulls were playing the Utah Jazz in the NBA Finals vying for their 5th Championship. The Bulls had a 3-2 lead in the series and I was watching game #6. This series had been incredibly thrilling because of how competitive and close the games had been. Game #6 was no different. The game was back and forth the entire time. Just as one team seemed as though they'd pull away, the other team would come roaring back. The Utah Jazz had never won a championship and thus they were incredibly hungry. They were fighting with all they had to take down the Goliath that was the Chicago Bulls. They had to win this game and send it to a final game 7. The sequence I want to talk about happened in the final minute of the game. The score is tied at 86 with about 40 seconds left and the Jazz had the ball. Their all star point guard, John Stockton brought the ball up the court and then made a beautiful pass to the rookie Shandin Anderson who tried to make a reverse layup but missed. The Bulls grabbed a rebound and quickly called a timeout.

During the timeout it was an interesting sight as Michael Jordan took his seat, leaned forward and sat fixated on something out on the court. He was looking near the top of the key but you could see that where he was looking, there was nothing there. He just stared at that spot with and intense look in his eye while he chewed furiously on his gum. It was an awkward sight as the entire Bulls bench was sitting there and no one was talking. The Coaches were in a huddle furiously working out what the play was going to be. Now everybody knows what the play is going to be. Give Michael the ball and get out of the way and hope that he can bring home another title. That whole time Michael just sat fixated and focused on what seemed to be nothing out on the court.

The Coaches then huddled up the team and laid out the play and just before the time out was over, Michael leaned over toward his teammate Steve Kerr, who is today the highly successful coach of the multiple champion Golden State Warriors and said,

"Stockton is coming off of you to double team me...Be Ready!"

"Kerr responded, "I'll be ready!"

The timeout was over and the Bulls made their way onto the court.

Steve Kerr brought the ball up and passed it to Scottie Pippen just left of the top of the key. Pippen held tight as Michael weaved his way around where Pippen literally handed Michael the Ball. Pippen then ran down toward the baseline to spread the floor and Michael stood with the ball as Bryon Russell, who was tasked with guarding Jordan shadowed his every move. Steve Kerr had now moved to the top of the key where John Stockton was guarding him. Stockton never took his eyes off of Michael. As Michael began to make his move, he went to his left and Stockton made a decision. He decided to stop guarding his man and he quickly moved to his right to double team Jordan. This was exactly what Michael said he would do. Just as Stockton made his way over, Michael continued to his left and then suddenly faked up a shot! Both Jazz players guarding him were fooled by the move and Michael stepped between them and passed the ball to Steve Kerr who was now left alone standing near the free throw line. Kerr caught the pass, squared up to the basket and I guarantee at that moment he was hearing Michael's words echoing in his mind: "BE READY!" He then took his shot...SWISH!!! He nailed it and Bulls ended up winning their 5th NBA Championship!!!

As I sat watching the celebration on TV suddenly I remembered the sage words Michael shared with me the day I met him:

"I think about what it is that I want to do. When I can get a clear picture in my mind of what that is, when I can see it happening and when it feels right in my heart it really helps me make it happen in my life."

It was then that I realized when Michael was sitting on that bench during the timeout seemingly staring out at nothing he wasn't focused on the empty court. He was focused on what was taking place in his mind! He was visualizing what was about to take place once the timeout was over. He saw the play unfold in his mind! That is why he was able to tell Steve Kerr to be ready. He knew he'd be double-teamed. He knew that Stockton would stop guarding Kerr to do just that. He knew that would leave Kerr open. So during that timeout, on that bench he shared his vision with his teammate. He told him to "BE READY" to step up and take the shot. I love that as a strong metaphor for life!

Each of us need to "BE READY" to step up and take our shot in life when the opportunities come. Therefore, we must diligently prepare ourselves for those special moments. The focus should be on taking the best shot possible and not on whether the ball goes in or not. For once the ball leaves our hand it is out of our control. Sometimes it goes in and sometimes it doesn't. Can you live in that moment knowing you did all you can when the moment comes? For therein lies the quality of our Performance and how we experience the abundance of what our lives can be. True fulfillment and true happiness come from the trying and from our journey towards excellence.

Another reason I love talking about this story when discussing the power of vision, is for what it represents in terms of uplifting not only your performance but the performance of others. Although the Bulls were getting better and better each season during Jordan's early years, they just couldn't seem to get to the Championship round. They kept running into the Detroit Pistons who had a rule when they played the Bulls. It was very simple and specific. They called it "THE JORDAN RULE." This rule was created in essence to let the world know that the Chicago Bulls will not defeat us if they solely rely on MJ. Therefore, whenever Michael had the ball they put the teams defensive focus on him and if he drove the lane they were going to knock him on his Ass! If the Bulls were going to beat them there would have to be a major contribution from the rest of the team. The problem was, that contribution was lacking. So what did the Bulls do? They fired their head coach, a guy named Doug Collins. This was a very controversial decision at the time because Chicago loved the fiery passion of their Coach and fans were truly upset. It didn't help matters with whom they replaced him with. The new head coach was the assistant and a guy at the time that most had never heard of, his name was Phil Jackson.

One of the first things Coach Jackson did after being named the head coach was he called a private meeting with Michael Jordan. During that meeting, Coach Jackson point blank asked Michael a question:

"Do you understand who you are to this team? I may be the head coach but you Michael, you are the leader and the reason we are not Champions is because of you."

This was a bold thing to say to not only the best player on your team but also one of the best to ever play the game. Michael Jordan is highly competitive and this statement really upset him so he got up, stormed out of the office and slammed the door!

A few weeks later Michael came back.

"I don't like what you said to me" he exclaimed to Coach Jackson. Then the Coach replied, "well you stormed out of here before I had a chance to finish what I wanted to say! Michael, you are without a doubt the most talented basketball player I have ever seen but the problem is you don't make the people around you better. The team stands around in awe of you not knowing their role. These are NBA basketball players and they have talent and something to contribute. If we could begin to play as a true team, where everyone understands their role and does it to the best of their ability then we will be unstoppable. Don't worry about winning and losing or championships. Make it about how we play this game! If we play as a TEAM then I guarantee, with you as our leader the Championships will come!" So what did Michael do? He changed his game and began to focus on making the people around him better. The result: 6 Championships in 8 years!!! And what if Jordan hadn't retired in the middle of it all? Well, we might be talking today about 8 in a row! But it was during the 5th Championship where it all came down to Michael's ability to see how that play would unfold and realizing that he couldn't do it alone. The rest is history and his words will always be with me:

"I think about what it is I want to do. When I can get a clear picture in my mind, when I can see it happening and when it feels right in my heart, its always helped me make it happen in my life!"

To establish a clear vision is a way of taking control of who you want to be and how you're going to create it. I always say in my presentations that the best way to predict your future is to create your future. This starts with a thought. Our thoughts are things. They matter more then we realize. They say on average we have around 70,000 thoughts in a day. Now I have no idea how "they" came up with that number but in my extensive research I have seen it many times and the reality is that 90% of those thoughts are the same thoughts we had yesterday! Therefore, we become stuck in a pattern that limits our experience of life. Having a "VISION" of our future can firmly place our minds in the creative mode and then we will begin to seek out solutions to actions that will help make it real. The vision alone can break us from the cycle of repetitive thoughts that create the same result of experience. For what is it that holds us back? Why do so many seem so stuck in life? Each thought has its power. Anything you give your attention to you give life to. This truth leads us to the understanding that we must be the directors of our own lives by first and foremost directing our thoughts towards the creation of what we want our experience to be. Over time our minds have changed and developed and some things were gained while others were lost. There is an intrinsic value to understanding the power of what has been there from the start. What if who you are today is absolutely enough to create your best life? What if all you need you already possess? Allow me to share a poem that has had a significant impact on my life:

"The greatest poem ever known
Is one all poets have outgrown:
The poetry, innate, untold,
Of being only four years old.

Still young enough to be a part
Of Nature's great impulsive heart,
Born comrade of bird, beast, and tree
And unselfconscious as the bee—

And yet with lovely reason skilled
Each day new paradise to build;
Elate explorer of each sense,
Without dismay, without pretense!

In your unstained transparent eyes
There is no conscience, no surprise:
Life's queer conundrums you accept,
Your strange divinity still kept.

Being, that now absorbs you, all
Harmonious, unit, integral,

Will shred into perplexing bits,

Oh, contradictions of the wits!

And Life, that sets all things in rhyme,

may make you poet, too, in time—

But there were days, O tender elf,

when you were Poetry itself!

-Christopher Morley

I would like to share with you why this poem is so significant for me. I have been working on and researching for this book for so long that when I started I had two young children. My son Jack was 8 and my daughter Gracie was 6. Today as I write this portion of the book those two young children are 18 and 16 and I have two more: Adeline is 2 and Molly is 3 weeks old. My children are the greatest part of my life & the greatest gifts of my life. They are without a doubt what I am most grateful for and being a Dad will always be the most important thing I will ever be. When my daughter Gracie was little she and I used to have tea parties. It is a memory I cherish for those moments were magical. One Saturday afternoon when Grace was about 5 years old she came to me and asked when our next tea party would be? We hadn't had one in awhile and she really wanted to. I looked at my calendar and it turned out that Monday could be a possibility. I was going to be speaking locally and would be home by noon and Gracie, who was now attending pre school would also be home by noon. So I suggested we do lunch on Monday at noon and then could have another tea party. Grace was so excited she began that very moment to get things ready! Getting this set up was no easy task because our Tea parties did not just consist of she and I. Grace insisted that all her American Girl dolls be present as well and Grace owned 6 of them! We had bought a little tea table with chairs and an actual tea set for our parties. Grace was so excited and our plan was in place.

When Monday rolled around I awoke with a bad cold. One of the challenges in being a professional speaker is there really are no sick days. If you are sick and you don't show up for a presentation you don't get paid. Not to mention the client will have an audience sitting there with no one to present. I had to muster up the energy and do the job I was hired to do. I got thru it and it went well but when I got home I was certainly in no shape for a Tea party with a 5 year old. Once I arrived back home I had about 30 minutes before Gracie would be back. I went straight to my wife and told her I was sick and that I needed to go upstairs and get some sleep. I asked her to let Grace know that I wasn't feeling well and that I couldn't play and have a tea party today. "I'll make it up to her" I exhaustingly said. My wife said to go on up and get some rest and that she'd take care of it. I immediately went upstairs and climbed into bed. I was almost asleep when suddenly I heard a ruckus downstairs as Grace was just come home from pre-school. She was running all over the house and making all kinds of noise. I was getting angry wondering why my wife didn't let her know I wasn't feeling well and was trying to sleep? Then without warning I heard our bedroom door slowly begin to open and Grace precariously peeked her head inside. I quickly closed my eyes and pretended to be asleep. I was hoping if she saw that I was sleeping then maybe she'd go away. I know this was wishful thinking but I had to give it a shot! I began to hear her footsteps entering the room. I thought to myself, "Don't open your eyes, if she thinks you're awake she's gonna want to play. Just pretend like your sleeping and maybe she'll leave." But then I noticed her footsteps stopped and the room was eerily quiet. I started to silently panic wondering what she was doing. I figured I better check so I very sheepishly opened up my left eye and was stunned because her face was right in front of mine. She looked deeply into my eye and said, "Dada, you don't feel good?" I replied in an overly tired way, "No, I'm sick." She then quickly jumped into the bed next to me, pulled the covers up to my chin and began very lovingly patting the top of my head as she said, "You go sleep Dada...just go sleep."

At that moment, a feeling of pure love washed over me. It was such a sweet and compassionate thing to do and in a matter of moments I was sleeping. My daughter was able to naturally empathize with me, connect with me and unconditionally love me. She understood that tender loving care was what I needed and without hesitation that is what she gave. This story illustrates that each human being has the beautiful qualities that give and sustain life. We have the ability to love, to show compassion and to connect to another. Over time we can lose sight of this as it gets buried underneath our doubts, our insecurities and our pain. If we can reconnect with that poet that lives deep inside our heart and our spirit, we can better understand our purpose and our ability to make a beautiful difference in the lives of others. When we choose to give of our love and our compassion, we experience the fullness of our lives. This happens because our love works through us. As you begin to take time to utilize the power of imagination and the art of visualization to "see" the life you want to create and the person you are striving to become, remember that your authentic self is already within you. Some things don't need to be created; they just have to be remembered. This step in the formula is key in helping you BELIEVE that your extraordinary life is attainable! So put your mind to work so that you become ready and inspired to take ACTION on behalf of your dreams.

During my research into the 2nd step, "BELIEVE" something very familiar came up: VISION BOARDS. Vision boards are simply taking the idea of visualization and making your "vision" or "goals" into something tangible that you create. I remember back when I was introduced to this concept by my parents during my senior year of high school. My goal that year was to become the state champion in cross-country. My mother had a poster board made up by a professional artist of me crossing the finish line as the Illinois state cross country champion for the year 1984. It was hanging above my bed one October day about a month before the actual race. The problem was I had nothing to do with the creation of it. I had no ownership in the vision. (I finished 2nd by the way) After I read about the potential power of these Vision boards I decided I wanted to do them with my two oldest kids. I thought this could be a neat way to test out the concept. So off I went to the HOBBY LOBBY and purchased two huge poster boards, one for my daughter (9 years old) and one for my son (11 years old). I brought them home and placed them in the front room where they sat for a couple of weeks. (One thing I have discovered in life for attaining success is that "follow-through" is key. Far to often I have had a great idea that just remained a great idea. When you don't take action on your ideas or visions they remain nothing more than just an idea) So, there the poster boards stayed, day after day as a daily reminder of my on going apathy. Then one day I was at the Barnes & Noble bookstore with my sister and my kids. My sister told her niece and nephew that they could each pick out one thing that she would buy for them. My son bought a Lego Star Wars video complete with a mini Yoda Lego figure. After an exhaustive search, my daughter came walking up with an item from American Girl that was some sort of arts and crafts project. When we got home, she came to me and asked in the best sweet little voice that she could muster, "Daddy will you do this with me?" Although at that moment I really wasn't up for it, I knew I just couldn't say no. We sat down in the kitchen, cleared away the dining table where we gather for our meals and began to unpack the contents of the box. I had no idea what this project was until we started to lay all the items out. As we did I began to realize this was not going be a simple undertaking so I decided to make the best of it. I went and put some classical music on and we lit a candle and created a peaceful environment.

The contents of the box began with 5 big cardboard letters:

D-R-E-A-M! It was then that I realized what this project was. We were to create and decorate these letters with my daughter's dreams and aspirations, making the letters come to life. We had beads, ribbons, stickers little special sayings and decorations. The first thing we needed to do was decide what my daughter's main dream was. So I asked, "Gracie, what do you dream of becoming when you get older?" She thought deeply for a moment then said quite seriously, "I want to be a professional dancer!" I said, "That sounds like a fantastic dream! Now you need to write that down on this special note card that we will place on the D." We began to work diligently decorating each letter together with all kinds of contents from the box. We had so much fun as Gracie directed the show and I did as I was told. We cut ribbon, pasted different sayings to the letters and glued little knick-knacks wherever she fancied. Each letter was unique and beautiful. As we worked, we talked about the many hopes and dreams in my little girl's heart. Her dreams varied from being a dancer, a veterinarian and an actress. I talked about my childhood dream of wanting to be a baseball player. The connection I felt with my daughter for those few hours was profound. Once the project was complete, we turned off all the lights, brought the candle closer to the letters and she posed in front of her DREAM project. Then it hit me, "This was my little girls VISION BOARD!" All her hopes and dreams were prominently displayed where she could see and think about them every time she looked at the word "DREAM." That word and her project now sits on the wall above her bed and every morning when she wakes up and every night before she sleeps she is reminded of her dreams, her hopes and her goals and maybe, just maybe she thinks about her Dad and the special time we had putting it all together.

The Legend of THE GOLDEN BUDDHA

In the temple of Wat Traimit, which is located in Bangkok, Thailand sits on an amazing and beautiful statue known as "THE GOLDEN BUDDHA." It weighs 5.5 tons and is pure gold estimated to be worth somewhere around 200 million dollars. The GOLDEN BUDDHA was not discovered however until 1957. According to legend, back in the 1700's the Burmese were set to attack Thailand and take over its land. The monks anticipating this decided to protect its most precious Buddha by covering all the gold with a thick layer of stucco, which was painted with pieces of colored glass thus making it appear to be nothing more than a worthless clay statue. The attack ensued and the statue remained behind among the ruins attracting very little attention because on the outside it looked to be worthless. (It was believed that all the Monks who knew the statues true identity were killed in the attack.)

Then years later in 1801, Thai King Rama the 1st established Bangkok as the new capital city of the Kingdom and commissioned the construction of many temples. Once the temples were created he then ordered that various old Buddha images be brought to Bangkok from the ruined temples around the country.

Some twenty years later Rama the 3rd had the statue, which was still covered in clay, be installed as the principal Buddha image in the main temple within Bangkok. After some years this temple began to fall into disrepair and was closed. It was then that the statue was moved to its present location in 1935. Since this location did not have a building big enough to house the statue, it was kept under a tin roof for 20 years as seemingly just an old relic made of clay and appearing to be worthless.

In 1954, they felt the Buddha, although made of clay was still an important part of Thailand's history. They decided to construct a building big enough to house it. Then in 1955 during its final attempt to lift it from its pedestal to move it into its new dwelling the ropes broke and the statue fell hard to the ground. At that moment, some of the plaster coating chipped off, allowing the gold surface beneath to be seen. All work in moving the statue stopped so they could remove more of the plaster to see what was underneath. It was then that the magnificent "GOLDEN BUDDHA" was discovered!

What I love about this legend is its relation to us as human beings. We are this story. I believe we come into this world as beautiful, magnificent and wondrous as pure Gold. We are priceless. Over time we begin to cover up that beautiful essence with our doubts, fears, insecurities and pain. Before long, the beauty we came into the world with is completely hidden, covered as if by a shell which we have constructed. We do so to protect ourselves when the reality is it only proves to make us feel lost. At times we try to paint over the shell with beautiful colors in the guise of possessions, accomplishments, trophies and accolades in hopes that it may convince others that our shell is beautiful. But deep down we feel lost and afraid while our true identity is still deep within covered in darkness. The beautiful Gold can no longer be felt nor seen. What we need is to find the tools to chip away at this shell. We need to BREAKTHROUGH! Why is it that we light up when in the presence of infants and very young children? I believe its because we recognize that we are in the presence of that beautiful gold. We can see it and feel it and are reminded of what we once were and can still be again. The key is, you must BELIEVE it's in there, then start the process of chipping away the façade and find your way back to it. What you come to discover is that YOU ARE truly magnificent and priceless! You are that GOLDEN BUDDHA!!!

STEP #3

Identify Your Team

The most significant way we experience the fullness and abundance of our lives is through our relationships. These relationships in essence become our TEAM. It is vital to be mindful of the people in our lives that we know we can count on. When I work with organizations on team building one of the most important aspects is the establishment of a strong connection and purpose among the team members. This is mainly accomplished by time and experience with one another. It is important for organizations to provide opportunities for this. These opportunities for experiences among the team need to be positive ones. For example, attending a baseball game together or having a nice dinner where the sole purpose is to have a positive shared and memorable experience. For example, one organization I worked with had recently purchased a few other companies who shared the same clients. They were trying desperately to create synergy among the various new team members in order to create increased profitability. This was slow going at first because the team members really did not know one another and thus the "trust" factor was very low. I noticed that the team members from the new companies were very similar personality types as the people in the main organization. I further knew that if they just spent some fun social time together they would mesh and gel and create friendships and genuine connections. I suggested some fun social events together that did not involve anything to do with their jobs. They arranged outings at sporting events, dinners, happy hours and even a night at a comedy club. Those fun shared social experiences began to bring the team together in very positive ways. Once these relationships began to be established as a "shared experience" they began to see great synergy organically being created.

One key component I have the organizations I work with initially develop is a "Shared Vision" that the entire team helps establish and implement. One of the powers that a shared vision has is it helps us build empathy & synergy with one another. This creates a deep connection that is lasting and meaningful. When people are on the same page in terms of the VISION of the TEAM then they can work together to collaborate and innovate to make the Vision real.

The true strength of the team comes from the strength of the relationships within that team. Teamwork is completely incumbent upon relationships but every team needs leadership. For leadership is about influence and if you are going to have a positive influence on someone you must first establish a solid relationship. The question becomes, "What are the keys to establishing strong relationships?" The first key came from something I read before I decided to get engaged. I had been dating Diane for about 6 months and our relationship was great and moving very fast. I was a bit anxious about the whole thing and confused about what to do. I loved her deeply but I was concerned with the fact that I didn't believe we truly knew enough about each other. One day, I was walking through the airport killing time before a flight when I happened upon one of those little convenience stores they have where you can buy a snack or a drink or a magazine. As I was browsing the magazine rack I saw a cover with a couple gazing deeply into each other's eyes, looking so in love and the caption read,

"How do you know if this is the one?"

I quickly grabbed the magazine off the rack and flipped to the page with the article. As I read, one of the things mentioned was a question: "How well do you really know each other?" This was intriguing to me because I never had really asked myself that question. The article went on to talk about an exercise you can do to discover some new things about yourself and your partner. It's called, "Recognizing the blind spots." I was intrigued.

In the article it said that you should ask your partner one simple question: "How can I improve?" The question itself was simple but that's not all there was to it. Once you ask the question, you are not allowed to speak until your partner has said all they need to say. When they have finished, all you are allowed to say is "Thank you" and then you must leave them for at least one hour. I remember thinking,

"What is the point of that? How is not being able to speak on ones own behalf and then having to leave going to help me figure out anything?"

I was perplexed yet willing to try. When I got home I waited for a nice peaceful moment. It was in the evening just after we had returned from a lovely dinner at one of our favorite restaurants. I turned to her and said, "Can I ask you something?" With some hesitation in her voice she replied, "Ok...what is it" I steadied myself and asked,

"How can I improve?"

She just stood there for a moment, then smiled and said:

"What are you talking about? You're the best thing that's ever happen to me! You don't need to improve."

It was very sweet but I was adamant when I said, "Thank you that's very kind but I want you to be honest with me because I'm trying to learn some things about myself so please answer the question, How can I improve?"

Suddenly she stopped smiling and just stared me down. She wasn't saying a word and I was a bit confused so I asked, "Well?" She just shook her head and replied,

"I'm not playing your little game because you know what will happen if I do. As soon as I criticize you, you're going to get all defensive and angry and then were going to argue. I'm not taking the bait." Now I was angry so I decided to explain the rules of the exercise.

"Diane, there is a purpose behind why I am asking you this. I am not allowed to speak at all as you respond. When you have said what you feel, all I am allowed to do is say "thank you" and then I must go away for at least an hour."

Her eyes opened wide and she seemed to say with great joy, "You mean you can't speak?" I said, "That's right." She said with a smile on her face, "Have a seat."

She then went into the kitchen and grabbed a bottle of wine and just one glass, for her. She came back into the room, poured herself a glass, thought for a moment, and then began a dissertation on the many ways she felt I could improve. She started with the obvious things that anyone who knows me knows is true.

"You're stubborn, you're argumentative and very opinionated and sometimes you talk too much!"

As soon as she began, I immediately started getting upset and although I couldn't actually speak, I was saying many things in my head. You see, I am one of those very "self critical" people and I am also very "self aware." You simply can't do what I do for a living and be good at it if you're not constantly trying to practice what you preach. I am pretty aware of where I could improve and I beat myself up quite a bit over it and that is why I don't take well to criticism. But I asked for it and was now yelling many things back at her in my own head! Then something dawned on me, I wasn't listening! After the first minute all I could hear were the angry responses in my head. I simply didn't hear what she had been saying and she had a lot to say. Once I became AWARE that I wasn't listening I began to calm down and focus on what she was saying. Then I began to hear her.

This was very revelatory for me because up until that moment my poor listening skills were a significant blind spot. I honestly thought I was a good listener. I was fooling myself! I didn't know until that moment that I was not a good listener. I knew what I needed to work on to make our relationship and in fact all my relationships better. I needed to work on listening. So I did what I normally do when I'm trying to learn something new. I immersed myself into the subject matter and read all I could about it. What I learned is that effective listening is actually a skill. It is something we can learn. I realized it was time for me to learn.

Listening is a major component to effective communication and as we all know effective communication is a key to having healthy and thriving relationships. What I didn't know is that effective listening is a proactive endeavor. I always thought of it as more passive. You sit back and listen...right? Wrong! We spend roughly 60% of our time listening during the communication process. On average it is believed we only retain about 25% of what we hear. When we listen we gravitate toward certain things that trigger our attention and understanding. First and foremost would be language. When we hear a language that we understand it obviously peaks our interest and understanding far more than a language we do not understand. It acts as a filter within our brains that is primarily unconscious to us. Other filters we have that affect what we pay attention to are the following: Attitudes, values, beliefs, culture & intentions. These unconscious filters actually create much of our reality for they inform what we pay attention to. Therefore, it is vital to become more aware of these filters. We need to learn how to bring them from the unconscious level to the conscious level of our thinking. This will always foster better understanding. The quality of your listening can be honed by focused attention.

Next time you find yourself in a crowded place with a lot of noise try to break down the sounds around you to see if you can locate its origin.

Think of each origin of sound as a channel and see if you can focus on a single channel at a time. This helps improve the acuity of your listening. Many experts believe we model our communication patterns off of our familial experience while growing up. One way to become more aware of our listening skills would be to look at how your family listened to each other during those important formative years of childhood. When you look closely enough at your own communication skill set, in particular listening, you may recognize some familiarity to how your parents listened to each other and to you.

When I looked closely at my own listening behavior I quickly recognized my fathers influence. My Dad is a very intelligent man with no patience for those who disagree with him. I remember feeling that I couldn't get my Dad to listen at times especially if I was trying to make him see things from my perspective. He seemed to get easily frustrated with my viewpoint and when it didn't align with his, he'd simply stop listening. That used to hurt because it caused me to feel insignificant. Then I realized as an adult that I act much in the same way toward those closest to me. I wasn't even aware of this for many years. The first step in change is being aware that change needs to happen. We cannot change what we don't acknowledge. We always hear of the importance of speaking from the heart but we also need to listen from the heart. This becomes more viable if we actually practice. We can practice listening from the heart thru deep focus on the individual that is speaking.

A great example of focused listening comes most often when someone is sharing a personal story. The power of storytelling can be so vital to the experience of effective listening. In fact, research shows that our brains are biochemically wired for stories. When we tell a story the listener tends to visualize and imagine what is taking place while drawing parallels from their own experience thus, creating ways in which to relate. Listening to a story makes the listening itself a very proactive experience. When we are proactive in our listening, we are able to comprehend and retain so much more then when we are passive. In my line of work, storytelling is key to my success. When we allow people to open up and tell their story, our focused listening validates not only what they are saying but it also validates who they are. This is why at my leadership retreats and company workshops we do what's called "The Hot Seat!"

THE HOT SEAT

The Hot Seat is a great tool to use within organizations to build strong teams. It is a way to communicate more effectively and listen proactively. What you do is take a member of the team and place them in a specified chair in front of the group. (I call it "THE HOT SEAT") Each member of the team is then able to ask questions of that member pertaining to the subject at hand. The team member in the "HOT SEAT" is encouraged to answer openly and honestly. In the beginning, once a team has been established, this is a great way to create a deeper connection among the team members. Truly getting to know the people who make up the team will create an empathic relationship, which is key to Peak Performance. This type of exercise is also very productive when we conduct a "needs assessment" for an organization. This exercise fosters openness and honest criticism. In order to discover what team members feel they will need to perform at higher levels, we need to afford them the opportunity to tell us what that could be. This also promotes a positive emotional connection. When the team feels a positive emotional connection toward each other it creates a synergistic environment. This will promote innovation and more importantly ACTION!

I believe in "Heroes" & "Mentors" for they can help show us the way by showing us "Their" way. Another example of one of my heroes is Warren Buffett. He is very much into the idea of "TEAM." He has a strict code when selecting his team members. It is a "criteria" that I feel is extremely important to share.

Warren Buffets 3 criteria for the type of qualities he would want from his team members:

1. Integrity. Saying NO to most things. Being aligned with who you say you are and what you actually do.

2. Energy/vitality bias to action

3. Adaptive Intelligence

Tools that will help:

-Write stuff down. What was I thinking? What's going on in my world and my life? It is the most valuable resource I have.

-Do not let your mind jump to far forward. What's the next step? Focus on the now & the very next moment.

-Balance family and career. How does a child spell LOVE? T-I-M-E. Do you live a life in tune with what you proclaim gives you the most joy?

Each and every team has to be made up of capable and motivated people who understand their particular role and how they contribute. When an organization learns how to put the right people in the key positions to implement the "Vision" then they are at a significant advantage for success. The most important factor is putting the compatible person in the correct role for what needs to be done. This can be considered an art form when it comes to putting together your team. Therefore, take the time to really get to know and understand the members of your team. Once you know the individuals you want on your team, it's time to get them to commit to helping you succeed. When I work with organizations and individuals on the concept of TEAM, I have them establish their support network. I'm going to take you thru the steps that will help you establish yours.

Make a list of support people in your life (Family members, extended family, co-workers, mentors, friends, neighbors, clergy etc.) Choose your Top Ten:

1.

2.

3.

4.

5.

6.

7.

8.

9.

10.

Everyone needs support in order to create the life they want. Share your "Dreams" & "Goals" with at least 5 people from the previous Top Ten list. Create a "contract" that will establish that you are asking them to be your "Support System" as you journey toward the creation and realization of your Goals and Dreams. By signing this contract they are committing themselves to helping you. This will hold you accountable while giving you the support you will need during your journey. The contract should look something like this:

I care about my Dreams & Goals.

I want to live my life to the fullest.

I am asking for your SUPPORT along the way.

Signature:_____ Date:_____

Once you get the people you desire to commit to being your "TEAM" and support network as you journey toward the creation of your Goals & Dreams, find ways to continually communicate with them so they can be a witness to your progress. Give them feedback along the way as to what they are doing that is helping and contributing to your success. Build trust along the way by allowing yourself to be open & transparent in what you try to do. Strive to be authentic along the way so that your TEAM can establish a meaningful connection with you. That very connection is what will fuel your desire to follow through with what you are setting out to do. These relationships you establish that are built on honesty, authenticity, empathy and compassion will lead to a genuine LOVE and that is where you will experience the truest abundance and beauty of your life!

STEP 4:

DEVELOP
THE GAME PLAN

This step is where the "work" gets done. This is where your daily activities, the choices and decisions of your life become the ACTION of your life. Before you can build your dream home you must first have an architect draw up the plans and the blueprint. I believe before you can live your best life you must do the same. We've talked about the beginning of the plan being the "vision" which helps you determine precisely what you are trying to achieve. Next we worked on getting your mind right and ready to BELIEVE that what you set out to do you actually can do. This focus and mindset will spark its creation. We then talked about the Team of people you must identify who share in your vision and commit to helping you along the way. This step in the process is all about the daily activities, habits and decisions begin the creation of the vision. The implementation of the GAMEPLAN is where the actions begins. One thing I want to make perfectly clear before we continue is that nothing will be accomplished without HARD WORK, DEDICATION & PERSISTANCE! These are the tried and true cornerstones of every great accomplishment. It is because of this hard work that makes it so worthwhile in the end. The first key to the implementation of your plan is the same thing a runner must do to have a successful race: GET OFF TO A GOOD START! In some cases just GET STARTED!

At the start of the race, runners jostle for early position and many times, if not careful you can get knocked down off the starting line. At times, competitors will try to move you off of your game plan. One must anticipate this and be ready if it happens. Therefore, to implement your game plan properly you must be aware that the real work will begin well before you find yourself on that "starting-line." The implementation begins in the preparation, the practice required to be ready to perform when the opportunity presents itself. This is where your planning becomes imperative. One of the first keys to achievement is to write down the goal. In step one, you figured out what you want and it is during this step you need to again be clear on what you want & why and then WRITE IT DOWN! There is plenty of research showing that those who write down their specific goals, plans or idea's are much more likely to achieve them. I think it helps because you become more consciously connected to what you want when you write it down. Then you must simply GET TO WORK!

I tell people all the time, "Your quest won't always be easy." What is it that will keep you motivated to do the hard work that it will take? It comes down to one word: PASSION! We know now that our Passion is fueled by our belief. Now comes the plan. The plan is "understanding" exactly what needs to be done to make it happen. Your team needs to be fully informed of the plan because they may have something pertinent to add. This is where I love utilizing the ideas of those around me. Getting everyone to "chime in" on what they feel would help could be very advantageous. I remember my Coach would have me think about and visualize when and where I would actually get started the day before an intense workout. This would begin to prepare me mentally and emotionally for the physical toll and sheer energy it would take. It was a technique that would inform me on what I needed to do to be ready. Information is power and that power could fuel some innovative ways toward achievement. First and foremost let me say once again: Write down your ideas. Get clear on what YOU feel needs to take place before you get the input of the team. This is important because it can help you easily identify the common denominators that may arise. When you have a common thread between you and your team about how something can work, then you have a shared belief. That shared belief will create high levels of motivation because multiple members of the team feel a sense of ownership in the strategy.

One of the keys to a successful game plan is specificity. The more specific and clear you can make the GAMEPLAN the easier it becomes to implement. When people understand exactly what is expected of them then they can set out to give you exactly what you're looking for. For example, if you look back to the opening story where I accomplished the goal of running a sub 4-minute mile, I reveal some of the GAMEPLAN therein. The track was 200 meters thus requiring 8 laps to reach a mile. If you break that down, it comes to 30 seconds a lap. In that respect, understanding that this was the pace made it clear and concise. I knew what I needed to do. I also knew that my teammate, Andre, would be setting the pace for the first half of the race. All I had to do was get set up right behind him and follow his lead. I then knew that when he dropped out there needed to be additional plans in place from that point. That is why I approached a competitor to be part of the plan. By asking Paul Vandergrift to work together after the half-way point was an insurance policy for the continuation of the pacing. This was all part of the strategy in knowing that by working together we could pull each other along to the accomplishment of the goal. This kind of fore-sight and planning is the exact things that need to be done to set one up to succeed. The more you are fully aware of what needs to take place the more you can properly prepare. Preparation is the key. Knowing how to prepare is the power. The daily routines of your life are either contributing to or diminishing from the quality of your life. Lets take a look at what we do on a daily basis and how it is creating the experience of our life.

Did you realize that the majority of leading scientists and doctors tell us that our bodies, with all its cells work together in order to create homeostasis, a balance, a self regulation? If you sleep well, if you eat the right foods, if you exercise, if you have healthy emotions and nurturing relationships then you have a better chance of creating a balance in your body and a healthier experience of your life. This Homeostasis is an "experience" and when you look at what goes into creating it they're many things we come to realize that we can control.

Reductionism is important in dissecting the root of the issue but holism is key to understanding its overall effect on our lives. We have to look at all things eventually in a holistic approach in order to understand any concern we may have on the entire "system" of our lives. Therefore, the body is just like an ecosystem and we are conscious beings living as part of this ecosystem. Just as the Universe, the tides, the constellations and the Earth as living organisms have rhythms to it so do our bodies. For example, have you noticed how at different times of the day you have more or less energy? This is called our circadian rhythm and it truly directs our moods, actions & behaviors. As I am writing this passage I find myself in the late afternoon and I am suddenly feeling very tired and run down whereas a few hours ago when I began this session I felt energized and vital. All that has changed is the time of day and yet I feel completely different. This is another example of how being consciously aware and "in the moment" can better predict the proper times to tackle certain tasks in your day. So for me, planning on doing something that requires energy in the late afternoon is a BAD IDEA! For the next few days I kept an "Energy Journal" and wrote down how I felt throughout the day to see if I could become more acutely aware of the rhythms of my life. This is what I found:

"ENERGY JOURNAL"

Synopsis of the week: I woke up 6:45am feeling tired at first but once I got up I felt pretty good. Energy level was moderate.

9am to 1pm: Had great energy in this time of the day. Felt vital and was able to get a lot done.

2-5pm: I felt very sluggish this time of time. It felt as if I had wet sand in my head. Had no energy and yet still had things to get done.

7pm-10pm: I began to feel more alive and energized. The thing I most noticed was my mood improved pretty dramatically. Toward the latter part of the evening I felt relaxed.

10:30-11:30pm: I began to wind down and got myself Ready for sleep.

By doing this journal I was able to notice how consistently I felt throughout each day. I had never realized before that my energy level really did fluctuate pretty dramatically from day to day. The one key to all of this stems from my sleep pattern. As long as my sleep was consistent then so to was the rhythm of my energy throughout the day. If I could keep to a "routine" then my sleep was restorative and I was giving my body what it needed to maintain the proper energy levels for my life. Our sleep needs to be healing to our bodies and minds. If our sleep is not consistent then we can run into problems. When I would disrupt this pattern I would notice it really did affect my energy on that particular day. This exercise began to jump-start my awareness that "routines" and "patterns" were a very important key to creating a well-balanced life. I was on to something. It began with sleep. The rhythm of my life is created and connected by many things. To be vital and healthy, rest is key but what I put into my body was just as important. It was time to get a deeper understanding of what I could do about the quality of my nutrition.

HEALTHY EATING

The first area I decided to focus on was my physical "well-being." I was about 20 pounds over weight, stressed out, anxious and exhausted all the time. I wasn't exercising consistently and I was eating a lot of junk food in order to comfort myself. I had also turned to alcohol to help me sleep. I found that a full glass of Port, used primarily as a dessert wine, had become my nightly medicine. Every morning I awoke feeling lousy after a night of restless sleep. Every time I looked in the mirror I just felt worse. I'm one of those people who gain weight first in my face so you can't help but notice it in every reflection. This would sadden me and so I would turn to unhealthy foods for comfort. My energy was low and so was my self-esteem but I knew at least in this instance that I could do something about it. A few years earlier I had injured my leg while running and I couldn't work out or run for months. I was afraid of the potential weight gain so I decided to get very strict about what I ate. I did this for about 6 months and in that time I had lost more weight then I'd had when working out at full force. This was a revelation to me. I learned then that what I put into my body played a significant role in how I looked and felt. This seems obvious but when I was young I could get away with eating whatever I wanted. Being a former world class runner I thought that I couldn't get into great shape without exercise. I was wrong. This epiphany was short lived however because once I started running again I went back to my old eating habits and within a few weeks I had gained 10 pounds!

I began to realize that as you get older exercise alone, will no longer keep the weight off. If you continue to overeat you will begin to add weight unless you are working out a couple hours a day. And to be honest who has time for that! So I knew what I needed to do, it was just a matter of making a decision. The word "decision" actually comes from the Latin root "to cut off from" so to truly make a decision it means you cut off from any other option. When it came to my physical health I had to once and for all decide to change my eating habits. This is not a diet this is a shift in lifestyle and how I began to utilize food to empower me physically, mentally and emotionally. I cannot emphasize enough the importance of truly "deciding" and what that does to the quality of ones life. I knew that once I headed down this path that I was going to take it 100% all the way and never hesitate or look back. I knew I could do it because I had done it before. I knew once I started and began to build momentum it would be a life changing moment. I'll use a popular poker term to help you understand, I was about to go "ALL IN!"

INVENTORY

The next step I took was I made a list of the foods I was eating, an inventory of sorts. I divided the foods into two simple categories: Those I felt were good for me, and those that weren't. The foods that fell into the negative column were things like: white bread, cookies, ice cream, coke, salami, cheese, candy, processed meats, bacon, pizza, mac n' cheese, potato chips, honey nut cheerios and of course alcohol.

After writing it down I was astounded by all the foods I was eating that were seriously not good for me. It became quite obvious as to why I wasn't feeling or looking better than I was. I was without a doubt, over-eating. The power behind the realization of this was that I knew I had the discipline to change. It was time to cut back on how much I ate while completely cutting out the foods that I felt were not good for me. Could I live without these foods? Could I actually cut them out of my life? I believed that I could but they needed to be replaced by healthier alternatives. So what were the foods I was eating that I felt were good for me? This is what I came up with: Fruits like pineapple, strawberries, blueberries & raspberries. Meats like grilled chicken and steak. Fish like salmon and tuna. Vegetables like spinach, broccoli, asparagus and carrots. Finally, eggs are something I love and a pretty good way to start the day a great breakfast. This was about the extent of my healthy intake. If I was going to get rid of all those negative calories they had to be replaced by something. I knew I had to discover other healthy foods that I could incorporate into my life. So that's what I did the very next day!

*The following are the foods I began to focus my eating around. I believe if you utilize these foods you will get down to your ideal weight. It is said that being in shape is 80% what we eat and 20% exercise. I was able to lose 20 pounds in 2 months by incorporating the following foods into my daily diet.

THE PROTEIN SHAKE

The first thing I did the next morning was I bought an industrial blender in order to begin creating healthy protein shakes filled with vegetables, fruits and protein powder. It was pretty simple. I bought a high quality protein powder from GNC and then hit the produce isle of my local grocery and loaded up on fruits and veggies. I would just throw in strawberries, bananas, blueberries, raspberries, spinach, carrots, a scoop of protein powder, a touch of honey and water. This blender I bought was so powerful all you had to do was crank it up and watch it all become a liquid meal. The large blender I had, made about 4 full glasses of this drink and I would down two of them and save the rest for the afternoon. This was how I started my days. It didn't take long before I noticed my energy begin to return. Now, I didn't do this everyday. I found that 2 to 3 times a week did the trick. I needed other foods that would help me start my day off right.

THE INCREDIBLE EDIBLE EGG

One particular food that I've always loved is eggs. A well-made omelet is one of my favorites and scrambled eggs were one of the first things I'd learned how to make for myself when I was a teenager. Eggs are a great source of protein. Eggs have numerous vitamins, including vitamin A, potassium and many B vitamins like folic acid, choline and biotin. In fact, very few foods share the same diverse nutrient makeup available in a single egg. Many of these are specifically for the health of the nerves and the brain and it's in the yolk that you'll find most of the vitamins and nutrients. Eggs are a beneficial source of some of the healthy fats that the body actually needs. So eggs are a great way to start the day, the only downside is the cholesterol found in them. This is why I don't eat them all the time but in moderation they are something I truly enjoy and is good for me.

HUMMUS

I stated above how I needed to replace some of the unhealthy foods I was eating with healthy alternatives. Well, I was lucky to find that in Hummus. You might not know much about hummus but it has been around a very long time originating in the Middle east. Several ingredients are used in making hummus but the primary ingredients are chickpeas and tahini. Chickpeas, which are more popularly known as garbanzo beans, are high-protein legumes. Tahini refers to sesame paste that has a strong flavor and thus is used sparingly. Other ingredients include lemon juice, salt, fresh garlic, paprika and olive oil. So now you know what's in it, what are the nutritional benefits? First and foremost, chickpeas are very healthy because they do not contain any cholesterol or saturated fats. They are also rich in protein. Chickpeas are also known to be effective in preventing build up of cholesterol in the blood vessels. They also help maintain correct blood sugar levels in the body. Hummus contains plenty of Omega 3 fatty acids, which are great for improving intelligence while maintaining a healthy heart. Hummus also contains the amino acids tryptophan, phenylalanine, and tyrosine which promote good quality sleep and uplift one's mood. So these are the technical nutritional benefits but in all actuality I love how it taste's! Another great thing about hummus it is what you can eat it with. I eat it with carrots, broccoli but mostly Melba toast. Although I gave up almost all bread I simply replaced it with Melba toast. Melba toast is simply thinly sliced bread that is toasted until it is completely dry. The caloric intake from Melba toast is MUCH less then that of regularly sliced bread which is filled with processed sugar.

FAT FREE COTTAGE CHEESE

We all have seen cottage cheese. It was something our mothers or grandma's would break out every now & again usually when they were on a diet. It looks disgusting to most people and thus many never give it a chance. But remember I knew I had to replace the foods I was giving up with something different. So one day while out for breakfast I got my usual 3 eggs scrambled with spinach and tomato mixed in and I would typically always get a side of crispy bacon. Well, since that was now no longer an option and a plate with just 3 scrambled eggs just felt wrong. So I asked the waitress, "What other healthy sides would you recommend?" And she said without hesitation, "Try some fat free cottage cheese." So I did and with a pinch of salt and was delighted with how good it was. Since that day at the restaurant, I eat cottage cheese about 3 to 4 mornings a week. Cottage Cheese is rich in protein and it can help you maintain and build and repair lean muscle mass. It is also a healthy source of calcium, which is important for strong bones. Remember though to choose fat free cottage cheese so as to avoid the saturated fat found in regular cottage cheese.

OATMEAL

One very important ingredient to a healthy eating lifestyle is fiber. When I looked at my eating habits it became glaringly obvious that I had very little fiber in my diet. I needed to find something that could help provide some of this. That's when I became reacquainted with a childhood favorite that I had lost touch with over the years, OATMEAL! It turned out that oatmeal was actually a comfort food from the past and it was good for me. So when I began to look into the health benefits to oatmeal I was pleasantly surprised by what I found. Oatmeal provides high levels of fiber, low levels of fat, and high levels of protein. It stabilizes blood sugar while it removes your bad cholesterol. Oatmeal contains something called "lignans" which protect against heart disease and cancer. It was amazing to me how healthy Oatmeal is because it also tastes really good! Another great thing about oatmeal is something my old college roommate used to call, "rib stickers." Oatmeal is very filling. It satisfies your hunger while it satisfies your taste buds. Once you have a bowl of steaming hot Oatmeal, it comforts you, satisfies you and your not hungry again for quite awhile.

TUNA

Some may think that tuna is a bit controversial as a healthy food because of the mercury found in it. But remember, I was looking for foods to replace unhealthy foods I would no longer going to eat and I have always enjoyed tuna. One afternoon at the grocery store deli counter I looked diligently for something to eat that would be good for me. I was giving up all those lunchmeats I used to enjoy and I wouldn't even allow myself to look at the cheese. I love cheese but I knew if I was going to eat well and lose weight and get fit then cheese could not be a part of it. As I began to give up hope perusing the deli selections my eyes became fixed on the tuna. I immediately thought, "I believe tuna is high in protein and pretty good for you." So I quickly "Googled" it and found that not only was I right about the protein but it had much more to it that was beneficial. It is loaded in nutrients and vitamins while low in saturated fats. When eaten in moderation, you can reap the healthy benefits while avoiding the negative effects of mercury. This was good to know because in my new style of eating, everything was now going to be in moderation. Tuna also has omega-3 fatty acid, which helps prevent high blood pressure and is very good for a healthy heart. Tuna also has an antioxidant called selenium, which helps improve the immune system. Tuna is also an excellent source of lean protein. I was so thrilled to see all of this because like I said before, I really enjoy tuna! Tuna has literally become my new "Pizza." What I mean by that is it has become one of my new favorite things to eat in moderation and it has much better health benefits!

THE MAINSTAY: SALAD

A big part of maintaining my new way of life would really be tested while I was on the road. The food lifestyle plan I have laid out is easy to do while at home. However, when I work as a professional speaker and self help consultant most of my clients are away from home. I can honestly relate to Johnny Cash when he sings his song about the road in "I've been every-where." I have been very fortunate in my 20 + years in this business to have presented in all 50 states and I have been to towns that most have never heard of. I love that part of my job though because I get to see America in a way that most do not. I also get to meet people from all corners of this vast and interesting country of ours. What I like the most are the different cultures you encounter out there and the various flavors that account for their uniqueness. The experience of the people themselves, the accents, the music, the architecture, the weather, the way of life and most of all the food, you truly get a taste of what it would be like to live there. I am a big fan of variety and fortunately this career provides a lot of it! One of the drawbacks though is It can be challenging to maintain a well-balanced life while travelling. At least that's how I used to feel. But once I had made up my mind to stick to my new way of life, it was incredible how one begins to find what one needs.

I began to recognize how often I would turn to food while on the road to deal with the stress and anxiety of travelling. I also began to recognize that when I would feel over tired, overwhelmed or exhausted that food would often times become my respite. Once I began to recognize the pattern, I was then able to anticipate these triggers. I began to realize how often I was eating when I wasn't even hungry. The food was providing something other then what it was meant for…COMFORT. But you hear all the time that when you are on the road and away from the "comforts" of home that your choices are limited. I say to anyone who believes that, they just aren't looking hard enough. In today's society you can always find healthy alternatives. Even McDonalds now has some healthy options. This is because of the epidemic America is in when it comes to unhealthy eating and the rise in obesity and diabetes. America is becoming an incredibly unhealthy place to live…for some. But if you choose to live a healthy lifestyle and to truly eat right, then America can be the right place to be. Seek and ye shall find. To understand what I found to make the difference I just need 5 letters: S-A-L-A-D!

One important decision while on the road is where to have dinner? Whether with clients or on your own, dinnertime proves to be an anticipated part of the day and where most people give in to the temptations of all the good eats on the menu. Dinnertime is when we begin to wind down from a long and busy day and when on the road it's as if you feel like you're on vacation where anything goes. Many times we will make excuses or simply feel we "deserve" to have what we want and thus we will forgo the healthy eating for whatever sounds delicious. We say things like, "I worked hard today and I deserve a treat." I always say, the food Gods don't care if you've worked hard today or if it's your birthday or your anniversary or whatever. The food you choose to put into your body will always have an impact regardless of the circumstances. It doesn't matter what day or occasion it is. For me, I stick to the choice I've made to eat healthy no matter what. For some that seems a bit harsh or stringent and that may be true but for me it works. I know that everything in moderation is a good thing and you hear this preached all the time but for me I like to stick to the momentum I have built. Staying true to the one way is what keeps it moving in a positive direction, which in turn helps me stay on course. For example, my favorite food in the world used to be Pizza. Every time I am around it now I decline and people will begin to question me. Inevitably, someone will say, "why don't you just have a slice?" Now for me, having one slice of pizza is much more frustrating then not having any at all. You see if I have one, then I want 4 slices. One slice of pizza would do nothing but cause me to crave more. If I don't eat it at all I honestly don't miss it. The satisfaction of Pizza has been replaced by a deeper satisfaction of being healthy and fit. I've also literally been able to train my taste buds and now some of my favorite things to eat are healthy alternatives like salad.

The great thing about salad is that it's practically everywhere. No matter where you choose to eat nowadays, one can get a healthy salad as an entrée and it can be very satisfying. I usually get a protein like blackened chicken or grilled chicken with it which helps make it a bit more filling. Another key to keeping it healthy is to not add tons of stuff to it. For instance, I won't put shredded cheese all over it. I will however, fill it with veggies like broccoli and carrots. Once you add some tomatoes, onions and a few croutons for some crunch, well then you've got yourself quite a nice meal. Oh yeah, be careful about the dressing. If you choose a creamy dressing like Thousand Island then you've added so many bad calories that you've negated the point in having the salad in the first place. I will usually go with a low fat balsamic or Italian dressing and then your all set. Because salads are literally everywhere, you can add variety based on which restaurant you choose. Many places offer a variety of salads that can be very pleasing. Remember, it's a great alternative and if done right it can be a very healthy way to go. It has become my main meal of choice when it comes to a night out on the road.

MY NEW COMFORT FOOD:
TEA WITH HONEY

I don't drink coffee. I've never liked the taste of it. I was introduced to it my freshmen year in high school after our 6am morning workouts for Cross Country. My varsity teammates who were all upper classmen drank it after the run to get themselves caffeinated for the school day ahead. One day they offered me some and I immediately spat it out. I understand that it is probably an acquired taste but I have no need or want to acquire such a thing. Years later in my twenties I discovered the vast world of Tea. I remember as a kid when I got sick my Mom would make me a cup of tea and it would soothe me. That same comfort was still there years later when I began drinking it again. The key ingredient though to making it such a pleasurable experience is HONEY! Adding honey to the tea gave it such a nice subtle sweetness and it was much better for you than sugar. Now on most afternoons when I start to feel tired and out of it and the cravings come, I will instead have a hot cup of tea with honey and it always hits the spot. Another benefit is that it always curbs my appetite and I no longer crave or need a snack. In trying to maintain a healthy diet while keeping fit I learned that snacking was one of the main culprits keeping me from being where I needed to be. It is simply amazing how unconsciously we snack. Feeling tired, grab some cookies. Feeling anxious, reach for the chips. Feeling down, ice cream will help. Feeling overwhelmed, chocolate hits the spot. The interesting thing is what all these snacks succeed at doing is comforting us in the short term while quickly raising our blood sugar and caloric intake. They also succeed at creating weight gain and a multitude of other health issues. When thought of in this light one quickly comes to the revelation that we have other ways to comfort ourselves that are much better alternatives. For me, Tea with honey really does the trick.

Tea has been a popular drink of choice for centuries. According to the Tea Association, it is the second most consumed beverage in the world second only to water. Our ancestors understood the overall health benefits of tea without the help of scientific research. They understood this based on their own experience and they passed it down to subsequent generations. That is why I remember tea being something Mom or Grandma would give to me when I wasn't feeling well. Today, we do have the benefit of scientific research and it is unanimously believed that tea has many health and weight loss benefits. Researchers and experts from The American Journal of Clinical Nutrition, The National Institute of Health and the US Department of Agriculture, have cited the many benefits of tea in your daily diet. They found that some of the natural compounds found in tea like polyphenols, are packed with antioxidants and potential health benefits. Tea can also increase energy expenditure and fat oxidation, which resulted in weight loss and helps maintain healthy body weight. Other studies show that regular tea drinkers have lower body mass indexes (BMIs) and waist to hip ratios, along with less body fat, compared with non-tea drinkers.

Drinking a variety of tea can have a myriad of health benefits. For instance, Green tea can help in halting the progression of certain cancers. Black Tea, which is my favorite, can reduce blood pressure while neutralizing the negative effects of high-fat meals on arterial blood flow. Darjeeling tea calms the mind, promotes healthy skin and strengthens bones. These studies show that drinking tea could help reduce significantly the incidence of stroke, heart attack and other cardiovascular diseases. Other research shows that the amino acid thranine and caffeine in tea are thought to strengthen attention, mood and performance. Amidst all the research that shows the many benefits of drinking tea, I find that there is a certain peacefulness that comes with stopping whatever I'm doing to have a cup of tea. This moment of relaxation and respite is very helpful in maintaining my balance and sanity in times of chaos and stress. Just sitting back and enjoying my tea for 15 minutes in the afternoon really eases my mind and gives me time to breathe. So the next time you are stressed or anxious or just tired and you find yourself unconsciously reaching for that unhealthy snack, SNAP OUT OF IT and grab a nice cup of tea. Don't forget the honey.

WATER:

This will be short and sweet. Water is simply what we all need to survive. Make sure it's clean but when it is, DRINK IT! Drinking water helps maintain the balance of body fluids. Our bodies are made up of 60% water. The functions of these bodily fluids include digestion, absorption, circulation, creation of saliva, transportation of nutrients, and maintenance of body temperature. Quite obviously you can see its involved in the homeostasis of our bodies and its overall balance. Water also helps energize our muscles and it helps keep our skin looking healthy. So when you're thirsty or when you're having a meal, drink water. It's simple, its effective and its good for you.

COLD SHOWER:

During a session I had with a client where I was training him with his platform skills, I asked what he does to relax. His answer was quite surprising: "Cold Showers" he said. I was very confused and surprised by this. Later that night I looked up the benefits to cold showers and was amazed at what I learned. Cold showers help create a stronger and more robust immune system, which can help you fight off sickness. Cold showers can relax the muscles and improve circulation. Cold showers can protect your skin and hair by not stripping it of their natural oils because the cold water closes pores, which tightens the skin. Cold showers can create a cold shock, which increases your heart rate and oxygen intake, which makes you more alert and energetic. Since cold showers make the blood flow faster through your body to maintain the ideal body temperature, they are beneficial in reducing inflammation and can potentially prevent cardiovascular disease. Cold showers are great for relieving itchy skin. I have been taking cold showers now for over 3 years and I have noticed that I am healthier and more energized because of them. Try it sometime you just might like it!

Success or failure in life is not ONE monumental decision or action rather it is the accumulation of all the decisions & actions, big & small as they connect together to create your experience. Many of these actions and decisions are directed by the unconscious. Since this is true, we need to create as many "Healthy Habits" as possible. Becoming more mindful of what we can control will help us do this.

THE MARSHMALLOW TEST

Years ago at Loyola University Chicago in a psychology class my sophomore year I remember studying an experiment known as the Marshmallow test. What they did was take 3 and 4 year old little kids and placed them in a high chair with an empty tray before them. They approached the little kids one at a time and brought them a Marshmallow and held it out in their hands and said, "Look what I have for you. It's a Marshmallow. I am going to put it down here on your tray. You can have this Marshmallow and eat it right now if you'd like. I have to go outside the room for a few moments but I'll be right back. If you don't eat the Marshmallow before I get back then I will give you another one! You can then eat both of them. If you eat this one before I get back then I cannot give you another one." They had hidden cameras set up to catch every move as they proceeded to exit the room. The cameras were rolling as they recorded what the children did next.

As you might guess, about 90% of the kids took no time at all and immediately ate the marshmallow as soon as the adult left the room. Some didn't even wait until they left. A few of the kids however, about 10% did not eat it right away. They wanted to wait and get an additional marshmallow once the adult returned. What's fascinating is recording what they did to accomplish this. They would distract themselves in order to keep from eating it. The first parallel the researchers noticed is that the children would deliberately not look at the marshmallow. Some would bury their heads in their hands or focus on something else in the room. One particularly stubborn child just stared directly at the marshmallow and seemed to will himself not to eat it. Whatever the case may be, the 10% of the children who succeeded in getting a second marshmallow did so by shifting their minds focus onto something else in order to delay gratification. This "delayed gratification" is the cornerstone to self-discipline. Self-discipline is one of the key tenets to success later in life. When the researcher came back and delivered the second marshmallow to those who had earned it, you could see the look of joy upon their faces knowing they had just accomplished what they set out to do. Then watching them enjoy their two marshmallows was inspiring. They seemed to relish in it! The question we must each ask ourselves is, "What would I have done?" I know for a fact that I would have gobbled it right up in an instant. This understanding of my own behavior can help me learn what I need to do to navigate myself in the present toward future success. I need to work on my own self- discipline. This idea of self-discipline and delayed gratification is a key to the implementation of the Four Minute Formula. It's called the implementation of the game plan. When you implement the game plan be ready to work your ass off because it won't be easy!

ACCEPT FAILURE!

One of the keys I have found to creating peak performance is the ability to accept failure. First off, we need to take away the stigma of the word and if you can't do that then we need to call it something else. What if you could train your brain to not focus on success or failures but rather results? By reframing what success or failure actually means can dramatically change the way you feel as you attempt to create a specific result. Ideally we are looking to create something we are happy with, something that will provide the impetus to keep going. It is the journey and the quest where actual changes are taking place in our lives. Sometimes the key to improving performance is to take focus off of the result and put it on the actions and choices that led to the result. It can help at times to work backwards from the result.

Carolyn Dweck of Stanford did some fascinating research on fixed mindset or developmental growth mindset. Fixed mindset example: "I'm not a MATH person." Belief in that fixed mindset excuses me from even trying to figure out math problems. Neuro-science has shown that the brain is very malleable and adaptable to learning and developing. Therefore, we are able to prepare ourselves for success by understanding and implementing the habits that can create it. Just as in the Stanford study where Ms. Dweck found that the students interested in learning and had a growth mindset were the ones who had the most success in high school and beyond. I believe if we are interested in learning how to be a better version of ourselves then that growth mindset will trigger decisions to find ways to do just that. With a growth mindset we can begin to focus on the things that we discover in our daily lives that lead us toward solutions, results and fulfillment. How do we know how we think? How can we discover which mindset we hold? Pay close attention to where you put your attention. Become aware of your minds focus and what experience its creating for you. Try not to attach to any particular thoughts just try to become aware of them. These are all important elements to discovering the world you pay attention to and how that in turn creates much of what you experience.

ACTING "AS IF"

There is an old proverb I've always loved: "Act as if ye have faith and faith shall be given to you." In other words, fake it until you make it. This idea is a concept that has been around for centuries. How exactly can it help us in our lives? I began to ask myself, "Where do people most commonly learn to act "as if?" As I pondered the question I realized that actors have to utilize this concept quite a bit. When they are playing a role and pretending to be someone they're not, they have to literally act as if they are that character. I realized what I could do to help me delve more completely into this ideology. I was going to take an acting class!

Living in the Chicagoland area I figured there had to be ample opportunities for those seeking acting lessons and as I looked thru the Chicago Reader it didn't take long before I came across an ad for "THE SECOND CITY" school of improvisational acting. There it was! I was so excited so I enrolled in the next round of classes. The first class was held at the legendary "SECOND CITY" where I had seen many shows and some pretty amazing talent over the years. People like Steve Carrel, Tina Fey, Stephen Colbert and the best of them all, Chris Farley! They had an annex a few levels up with a mini version of the actual main stage. It was a Wednesday night and there I was with a much younger group of aspiring actors and comedians. I wasn't looking to become a member of "SECOND CITY" I was just on a mission to create better stage presence as a speaker and to see if I could learn to be more open and spontaneous on stage.

The very first message that was hammered home to make improvisation work was you have to say "YES AND" to any and all scenarios that arise. I found this interesting especially when I began to think about the impact that this idea might have on my life. What if I applied this concept to my actual life? Now remember, the reason I am doing all of this is to improve my chosen craft as a speaker and to see if these ideas can work in a practical way. With this in mind I realized quickly that it wouldn't be prudent or particularly worthwhile to always say "YES AND" to every aspect of life. But I did make the connection that being more positive when it came to the circumstances of life would probably be more beneficial. When you are trained to say "YES AND" to whatever scenario arises it forces your mind to search for possibilities that might work. I realized that this sparked my creativity and opened my imagination. Once that occurred I found myself coming up with idea's that could contribute to the scene to make it richer. This was a revelation to me because in essence that is exactly what I am striving to do with my life. I want to have a richer more satisfying experience. Maybe I wasn't as truly optimistic as I thought? In actuality, I had become more jaded then I'd realized and thus more closed off without even acknowledging it. To be more open, more willing, it will take a focused and conscious effort just like this "YES AND" exercise did in this class. With enough concentrated effort it could become who I am again. I say "again" because I believe at some point in our lives, usually when we are very young. we naturally live in this way. Inevitably, life intervenes and we begin to be more guarded, less trusting of ourselves as well as others and closed off. For many of us, I believe we can't even see it happening. We become transformed over time and not fully aware that it has taken place. When your conscious mind is focused on trying to move things forward, you need to adhere to the "Yes And" philosophy. As soon as someone didn't, it brought the scene to a screeching halt. What I like about this concept is that it fosters collaborative attitudes and thus cooperative behaviors. This in turn produced a communal experience among the participants and you really had to listen to what was taking place. Listening became a very proactive endeavor and I never realized what an integral part this is to effective communication. To prepare us for this we did a few listening exercises that forced us to really focus and contribute.

The first of which was we stood in a circle, about 20 people total and as a group we had to tell a story. The rules were that each member of the circle could only add one word to the story when it was your turn in the circle. The goal was to first and foremost say something that would add to the story while keeping it moving forward. This required us to listen to each and every word and then anticipate the right word to add. I remember our story went like this:

(Position #1 starts the story with the first word and then each position added one word until our story was complete. Here's what we came up with. I was position #9):

"The-squirrel-ran-into-the-arms-of-a-schizophrenic-clown. She-didn't-understand-why-this-rodent-was-holding-a-crown. She-assumed-that-the-crown-was-for-her-but-she-was-mistaken. The-squirrel-was-furious-because-she-wouldnot-stop-fighting-with-the-voices-in-her-head-so-she-gave-the- squirrel-some-yummy-bacon."

That was the story and I remember it because it was recorded. Since we all had to concentrate and listen we were able to move the story forward and made it rhyme! I learned then and there that I really needed to work on my listening. I also learned that most of our listening actually happens with our eyes. Its how we say the things we say that have it's deepest impact on the communication itself. By focusing on each person as they added a word to the story, I was able to anticipate how I could keep the story moving along while adding something to it. Sometimes I had a chance to enhance the story with a word while at other times I could just keep it moving forward because that is what was needed for the story itself. My words in the story were: "schizophrenic, her and voices." This was an important lesson for me because it showed quite clearly that it's not all about me. Sometimes I will have my opportunities to shine but sometimes it's about setting up the opportunity for others to shine. I found that I needed to be doing a bit more of the latter in my life.

This reminded me of a time when I was at Loyola University Chicago in Father John Powell's (a pretty well known author) creative writing class. We had read a book as a class and were now discussing it. Father Powell was asking us for our opinions and I was so into the class that I was constantly raising my hand and adding my 2 cents. I was dominating the conversation and really leaving no room for other opinions. After class Father Powell had pulled me aside and in his tender way he basically said, "Eddie, sometimes you need to be quiet so that others could speak." He told me that there was a girl in class, her name was Rose and she was very timid and shy and never participated. Father Powell had noticed that she wanted to share something about the book but because I was going on and on, he could tell how intimidated she had become and thus decided against it. He then said something I've never forgotten,

"Eddie, you have a tremendous gift to inspire and tell a story and you can be incredibly persuasive, but sometimes you need to be aware of others and their need to be heard. That is why the good Lord gave us two ears but only one mouth."

will never forget that exchange and how it resonated with me. This is something that I still work on to this day. It's no wonder I became a speaker! I love to be the center of attention and boy do I have opinions (just ask those who know me best) but I needed to learn that as much as I like to shine, so to do others. When I began to exercise some empathy I came to realize that we all have a voice and the need to be heard and sometimes the gracious thing, the right thing is to listen and be inspired by the thoughts, feelings and opinions of others. I'm still a work in progress...but I'm getting there. Being aware is what helps me be better.

Our next exercise required us to actually do some scenes utilizing the "YES AND" philosophy. The idea is to keep building the scene by agreeing with the premise and then come up with your own improvised idea that will service the initial premise. The following is what took place:

There was a group of 15 of us that got on stage, facing the audience in a semi-circle. They told us we were going to do three-person scenes, in which they'd randomly call out three names from the group of 15 and we'd have to conduct a scene on the spot. It was very simple; the teacher would call three names to center stage and give you a setting (i.e. the zoo). Your job was to immediately come up with a character that would fit into the setting and begin interacting with your scene partners. It can be a daunting task to make something out of nothing.

The first three names were called out and I watched as they began their scene. The teacher gave them the setting of a "football stadium." Immediately, the first guy in the scene began practicing his field goal kicks and talking about how the game was "on the line." This was a pretty good start that fit the setting. The problem was the second guy in the scene, who decided to use this moment to bust out his exaggerated "Italian accent" for some unknown reason.

"Whadda-you guys a-doin on-a da foosball field? We got a-da pizzapies ta make!!!"

Needless to say, the other two people in the scene just stared at him slack-jawed with no idea of how to continue the football scene in a way that made any sense. The overdone Italian-accented pizza guy had singlehandedly ruined the scene. Quite simply, he had failed to use the idea of "Yes and." His approach was more like "No, but." The scene would have at least had a chance if instead he walked in portraying the coach giving his field goal kicker a pep talk with the game on the line. That would have made sense and allowed them to further the scene.

And that's when it hit me: I needed to save his scene-mates. I would embrace "Yes and" while helping to get their scene back on track. I walked to center stage and said:

"I am so sorry but Guiseppe here escaped from the mental institution this morning? I've got him, you all have got a game to win here!"

Mr. Italian Accent looked at me like I was the crazy one. The field goal kicker looked at me with a mix of relief and excitement and he took the scene from there. The scene ended up being a great example of what to do and what not to do. If you follow the rules of building, supporting, and saying "Yes" to someone else's idea, you can move forward with the improvisation. This turns out to be a great lesson for life as well. Positivity gets you places. Negativity stops you in your tracks and scene stealing is definitely a crime!

THE ONE KEY INGREDIENT
FOR SUCCESS

Some year's back when I lived in Chicago, I had an experience that always reminds me of the one key ingredient we all need to find our true success. It was a summer Saturday morning in the year 2000 and I was heading to the local health club to play some pick up basketball. The club I belonged to was called the Multiplex. The Multiplex had a few locations one in the city and one in a northern suburb called Deerfield that doubled as the Chicago Bulls training facility. It had been rumored that every now and again some of the Bulls players would show up to play some basketball at the downtown location where I belonged. I would go to this facility 5 times a week and I had never seen a single Bulls player. The pickup basketball games were fun because they were organized with a timer and a scorekeeper. This helped keep some sanity in the otherwise crazy world of pick up ball.

As I entered the club I could sense that something was off. To the right is a large open workout area filled with weights, treadmills, bikes and all kinds of exercise equipment. Next to this was a huge glass partition and on the other side a beautiful basketball court. The odd thing was, nobody was working out. Everyone was leaning up against the glass partition or had gathered around the court watching the pickup basketball game. I didn't pay it much attention I just made my way over to the signup sheet to get into the next game. At this club, the pickup basketball is so popular that they are constantly shuffling teams in and out so that everyone can play. It is very organized and like I said before they had a scorekeeper along with a timer, which was displayed on a huge wall mounted professional scoreboard. (I know it's pretty amazing for a health club.) I put my name down and I stood on the sideline waiting. As I stood and watched the action on the far end of the court, I noticed out of the corner of my eye someone down on the other end warming suddenly jumped and thunderously dunked the basketball! I thought, as I looked his way, "Who the hell is that?" To my amazement I recognized right away who it was. MICHAEL

JORDAN! I couldn't believe it! That's why no one was working out. They were all watching Michael as he waited on his chance to play. I quickly glanced back at the signup sheet and noticed Jordan's name a few above mine. My. Heart skipped a beat as I realized that very soon I'd be playing basketball with Michael Jordan!

A few minutes later the game we were watching ended and they called out the next 10 names on the signup sheet and two teams were divided up and took the floor. To my dismay, I realized I was not on Jordan's team. It was simply unbelievable to me that I would be playing a game against the greatest of all time!

We were awarded the ball first and my teammate took a jump shot and missed. Michael Jordan grabbed the rebound and quickly began running up the court with intensity in his eyes as he headed right toward me. I was our point guard so because I was already back near half court my job was to stop the fast break by stopping the man with the ball who happened to be Michael Jordan! As he raced toward me a million thoughts were racing through my mind. Instinctively, my competitive nature took over and I focused sharply on stopping him. As I back-pedaled at half court, Michael faked to his left and then like a flash of light dribbled the ball between his legs and went right. Being completely fooled I tripped over my feet and fell flat on my back. Jordan raced right past me unimpeded to the basket where he dunked the ball!!! As I laid flat on my back at half court completely humiliated all I heard were the sounds of laughter. Jordan then ran by me, pointed down and said sarcastically, "Nice defense." He was trash talking me!!! In an instant my humiliation and embarrassment turned to anger and revenge! You see, I am a very competitive person. Anyone who knows me well can attest to that. What is the one thing I can do better then Michael Jordan? I can out run him! I can outlast him! I have more endurance and I was still in great shape. So now all I was focused on was getting even, so in that moment I made it my life's mission to steal the ball from Michael Jordan!

I decided that I was going to double team him all over the court until I stole the ball from him. What a story that would make to be able to tell my grandkids one day that not only did I play basketball against the greatest of all time but that I stole the ball from him! This became my sole objective. So I began the relentless chase. Wherever he went on the floor I was right on him. The only problem was not only could I not get the ball from him, our entire team simply could not stop him. He was single handedly destroying us!

The score was now 22-7 with about 30 seconds left. We play until one team has 25points or until the clock runs out, whichever comes first. Michael had the ball along the baseline way back in the corner beyond the 3 point line. I had given up the double team a few minutes earlier because it was futile and I felt completely defeated. I could see what Michael was planning. He was running down the clock to take the last shot. Then I realized that this was my last chance to steal the ball from him and if I was actually going to do this there was only one way...I had to cheat. I was on the other side of the court as Michael was just dribbling the ball with his back to the basket all the way in the baseline corner. We had our biggest guy trying to guard him standing directly in front of him. I was all the way over on the other side of the court when I realized just how I could accomplish this. I could quietly and nonchalantly slip beyond the baseline, out of bounds and blend into the crowd of spectators watching Michael. I could then weave my way thru the crowd until I was directly behind Michael where he could not see me. I could then come from out of bounds and steal the ball from Michael, race down and make a layup before the buzzer sounds. I realized this wouldn't count but I didn't care. If I pulled this off I will have stolen the ball from the G.O.A.T. So I quietly slipped out of bounds beyond the baseline where the spectators were. I made my way along the baseline still out of bounds where Michael could not see me. There was now about 10 seconds left as I had successfully made my way to where I was now right behind him coming from out of bounds. With about 7 seconds to go I made my move. As I bolted from the crowd to steal his dribble from behind, he grabbed the ball and turned. At that moment not being able to stop I ran right into his ASS because he is 6'6 and I'm 5'8! His ass being rock hard caused me to bounce off of it and off my feet where I crashed once again to the floor and flat on my back. I watched from the floor as he would shoot a 3 point jumper, swish it as the buzzer sounded. He then, without hesitation turned toward me, again lying on my back while pointing an accusatory finger in my direction and with fire in his eyes he said, "I SAW YOU THE WHOLE TIME BITCH!!!" And he marched away. That's right, Michael Jordan called me a BITCH!

I will never forget that moment. That experience showed me first hand the power of ones drive and how it can fuel our success! Now, I am a very competitive person but I was no match for Michael Jordan. He simply would not be beaten in any way, shape or form. This is why he was so incredibly successful. He not only had a passion for winning he simply wouldn't accept anything less. This fueled his desire, which in turn fueled his work ethic. People who had the pleasure of playing with Michael Jordan will tell you that not only was he the most talented player they had ever seen but he was the hardest working player as well. Nobody worked harder than him. To be successful in any aspect of life we have to be willing to work hard for it. Nothing worthwhile happens without it. It is where your determination is born. This is where you earn your dreams! Now it is time to create and implement your gameplan. The following is a template I teach in my Goal Setting workshops to organizations to help them setup the game plan for creating the outcomes they desire. I've included it here in my book to help you do the same.

Goal Setting/Action Planning

A goal is an action-oriented target to shoot for within a specified time frame.

1. Components of a Well-Written Goal

- Start with the words "I/We Will" (connotes commitment)

- Follow with an Action Word (fix, changes, develop etc.)

- Specify the Expected Results (What is it that you want to accomplish?)

- State with no alternatives.

- Specify cost and a quantified output measure (include time & money)

- Set a deadline with a target date.

2. Sample Goal

We will develop an Action Plan for creating and holding a prevention event for all students on 1/18/19.

Test Against Guidelines

Must answer: "YES" to each of the guidelines to determine if you have a well-written goal.

Is the Goal?

- Conceivable: Can you see yourself doing it?

- Believable: Can it be achieved?

- Achievable: Do all participants have the skills to make it happen?

- Controllable: Do you need outside sources to help you?

- Measurable: Do you have a target date for completion?

- Desirable: Will it be a benefit to both parties?

- Stated With No Alternative: Be specific – no if's, ands or buts.

- Growth Facilitating: Will achievement of the goal be a positive force for solidifying partnership?

3. Write Down All Tasks

- Everything that needs to be carried out to achieve the goal.

- Let everyone present ideas.

- Have group leader record all ideas without evaluating/providing input.

4. Test Tasks Against the Goal

- Which ones are possible solutions, which ones should be eliminated?

5. Prioritize A Final List

- By order of importance with deadlines for completion of each task.

- Assign tasks to team members.

6. Follow Up

- Check to ensure that all tasks will be completed as scheduled.

7. Implement all Action Items

This is a comprehensive guide in helping you setup and begin implementing your game plan. Once you are set with the action plan...GET TO WORK!!! Remember that the difference of those who create successful results from those that don't comes down to who is willing to put in the work and who isn't.

STEP #5:

Prepare for the PAIN

One of the first things we need to ask ourselves when confronted with an obstacle in our lives is what is it that's holding us back? When we have conflict, especially internal conflict, we first must take a good honest look in order to understand its roots.

"Am I the one creating the conflict? Is this conflict something that is true or have I manufactured it?"

If I attach or bind myself to what is negative or unsatisfactory in my life than how could I ever feel satisfied? Yet we tend to do this to ourselves much of the time. Once you discover what you are doing that causes pain and discontent in your life ask yourself, "What will I do about it?"

Notice I said; "Will" instead of "can" because "will" means some form of action and "can" means some sort of understanding. We always need to be looking to ignite our passion so as to drive thru any obstacle that is external and let go of any obstacle that is within. This doesn't mean however that you won't experience some pain or hardship along the way. That pain and hardship, in my opinion are part of the process. It is the chance for you to define in your heart and mind how bad you really & truly want something. In other words, I'd like to juse a great quote from the character jimmy Malone in the classic movie: The Untouchables, "WHAT ARE YOU PREPARED TO DO?"

It seems as though our world is set up to try and make us feel discontent. This discontent is the fuel that keeps us wanting. This discontent can cause us to believe we are not good enough so we must change ourselves and or our circumstance. Sometimes the things holding us back are the thoughts and beliefs we have about a particular obstacle. If we believe the obstacle is just to big or overwhelming then we will lose our incentive and drive to do anything about it. This is the moment you discover whether or not you are truly committed to your own happiness & your own fulfillment. It's your Passion & Drive fueled by your belief that no obstacle is "to big" to overcome! It is your humility that will inform you that you have been the cause of much of your own pain. How you choose to practice or live your life on a daily basis will become your experience.

I was on a flight heading to Nashville to speak at a conference and I was watching one of my favorite musicians, Bruce Springsteen in his movie/concert "Western Stars" on my iPad when he said something that resonated with me:

"Sometimes you just gravitate to the pain, it's what you're used to. It's how you recognize yourself. It feels like home. It feels more familiar to you then love, so that's where you go. You don't know how to hold onto love but you know how to hold onto hurt."

Suddenly I realized that I was crying. Not only did I understand what he was saying, it had been my experience for much of my life. I began to wonder why? Why is the pain of my life where I recognize myself? I don't want to live in that dark place yet that's where my comfortable furniture seems to be setup. It's something deeply rooted in me and before I can begin to pull the weeds surrounding that root I need some awareness. Awareness is the beginning of transformation. Holding onto hurt is something I know how to do. I've become adept at it in a way that I don't even realize when it's happening. It has become a habit and a ritual in the way I have lived. This way of life is the destroyer of love. What do I do when the pain hits? What do I need to learn and put into practice in my life to cope? Let me share what I have learned in the following story.

One day that I will never forget is November 2nd, 2011. This was the day that my ex-wife asked me for a divorce. It wasn't a surprise because we had been struggling for quite some time. We were married for 12 years and from the very beginning, even when we dated, it was a rollercoaster. The last 3 years had been particularly rough. To be honest, there was a part of me that wanted a divorce too but I just didn't want to put my kids through that. We have two beautiful children and at the time Jack had just turned 10 and Grace was almost 8. I'm sure my ex didn't want to put them thru it either but she was done.

When night would come and it would be time for bed, after the kids were tucked away I would head down to my basement. Since she had asked me for the divorce, I had begun secretly sleeping down there as we began the process. It was done in secret because we hadn't told the kids yet. When it was decided we would divorce, I went to the bookstore to find whatever I could on the subject of divorce so that we could try and make this as painless and as smooth as we could. One of the things I had read is that you should never tell your kids something heart breaking like divorce around a major holiday. We had just passed my Sons birthday and Halloween and Thanksgiving was just around the corner. Then of course we would be in Christmas mode so we decided to wait to tell them what was happening. So they didn't know, but I was in a very lonely place and I was suffering.

The basement was cold and dark and as I would lay on an old futon in that musty space, I had a lot of time to think about my life and who I was and what had happened to our marriage. I very critical, judgmental and hard on myself. I would beat myself up over what mistakes I had made. I would relive an old pathology that felt very familiar. The negative thoughts and the dark feelings, I was used to this for this is how I had always been when it came to how I treated me in painful times. Then one night it just hit me, I didn't need to do this to myself anymore. I began to see how I was towards others in my life. From family to friends, I was very compassionate and forgiving. I was the kind of friend that when you truly needed something or someone then I was there for you. I am an incredibly loving and compassionate person when it came to others, I just wasn't that way toward myself. Why? In truth, I wasn't even aware of it until that moment in my dark basement. I really didn't have to be that way toward myself anymore. I could actually begin to move forward in my life. I was suddenly awake in the truest sense of the word. It was a moment of clarity. I could actually be compassionate, forgiving and loving to me. The moment that thought came into my being the emotions came over me like a tidal wave. I cried and cried and in doing so I began to feel as though I was healing from a deep wound that I didn't know existed until right then and there. It was revelatory and it transformed me and would change the rest of my life! What I had learned that night was the power of FORGIVENESS. It is so important in life to practice forgiveness. When others hurt us we have the choice to forgive. But what do you do when YOU HURT YOU? I have always been very forgiving of others. Some how I knew what a burden it was to carry a grudge or anger toward another. I just hadn't realized how opposite I was when it came to me. When we can't find forgiveness for ourselves, it can create a dark cloud that resides around our heart. Deep down it can come from a feeling that believes we don't deserve forgiveness. That feeling, can and will take away all your self worth. It can be devastating. True forgiveness can free you. It comes down to the simple truth that each of us deserve forgiveness. We are worthy of it and when practiced it will be transformative!

MOVING FORWARD

After some time had passed since my divorce and some serious soul searching had happened, I was ready to get out there and date again. It had been many years since I was single and I was pretty nervous for the whole prospect of starting over again with someone else. I really didn't even know where to begin. Where could I meet someone? The answer was simple...Online! Since I was last a single man some 14 years prior, the Internet had provided for the perfect forum to meet other singles looking to get together. The year was 2012 and there were two main online dating sites. So I joined both! Like Aladdin sang, it was "A whole new world." Each day you could look thru dozens of single women's pictures and profiles to discover someone that could be a good match. Once you found someone that might be promising you'd typically ask if they'd like to meet for lunch or a drink somewhere? This was the least intimidating way to get together and see if there was any chemistry or connection. Most of the time, Starbucks seemed to be the place they'd like to meet and ironically, I don't even drink coffee. This non-threatening first date gave each of you a chance to size one another up. In fact, it was very eye opening how much of a role the physical presence of someone plays in whether or not this connection could move forward. The photos that were shared on the site were one thing but real life was something completely different. In fact, in my experience most of the women I met up with had obviously posted online pictures that were from when they were much younger...it was obvious. I found most of it to be a waste of time. I had only one meet up that turned into another date out of the 9 women I met. So I decided to try something else.

One day while watching television I heard a song I have always loved called "This will be" by Natalie Cole. It was playing on a commercial for eHarmony. The song captured my attention and so to did the premise of the website. This was another dating website but it seemed to go a step further in helping you find a good compatible person to date. They had you fill out a questioner and a personality profile. They did this to gather personal information so as to hook you up with a "good fit." I liked this concept and in fact I have a workshop where I utilize Personality Profiles in my consulting business so it made perfect sense to me. After filling out the extensive personality profile I waited about a week until suddenly I had what was called a "Wink" from several women. This meant that they were interested. Next comes a "boiler plate" of questions eHarmony puts together to ask your potential match. This allowed us to discover, prior to meeting if there truly is some solid compatibility. After which, if there is you can give your number and call them on the phone. I went on four dates thru this method and only hit it off with one woman. We dated for about a month and then that petered out. I was about ready to give up when one lonely night I decided to take one more look at the site to see if someone sparked my interest. Someone did!

What caught my attention first was how beautiful her profile picture was. (I'll be honest, that's usually where it begins) but then what intrigued me was her profession. She was a vocalist and an accountant for a property management corporation. I thought that was interesting and I certainly wanted to learn more...so I sent her a "Wink." An hour later she sent one back! Now came the "boiler plate" questions. I decided I wasn't going to take that route. So instead I sent her a message (which you could now do because of the returned wink) saying:

"My name is Eddie, I'd love to get to know you better but I'm not interested in the website's boiler plate questions. I'd rather get to know you the old fashioned way by actually talking to you. If you're interested, here is my cell number, call me." I decided to take this more direct approach. 10minutes later, my cell phone rang! It was her!

We spoke on the phone that first time for over an hour and immediately I felt a connection. She was easy to talk to, interesting and kind. I found her to be very genuine and that is what impressed me the most. We spoke on the phone the very next night again for over an hour and a few days again after that. It was just very natural and I couldn't wait to meet her in person. At the same time I was apprehensive because when I met others from the website before, they didn't look like the pictures they'd posted. There was only one way to find out. So I planned our first date to go to a tapas restaurant in downtown Chicago. When I told her my idea she reminded me that the "cross town classic" was happening that same night and would I rather go to that? We had discovered in our numerous phone conversations that I was a big Cubs fan while she loved the White Sox. The "cross town classic" in Chicago is a baseball series where the Cubs played the White Sox. I had forgotten that was going on and I immediately thought, "What a great idea!" I was also very excited that she wanted to do that because it informed me that she was a sports fan like I was! So I was able to go online and get some tickets. Our first date was planned. Diane lived in Chicago on South Michigan Ave. When I looked up her address I saw there was a bar called "The Weather Mark" right across the street from her apartment building. We decided we would meet there first and then head over to the game. I was excited!

I arrived at the bar an hour early and had a beer waiting for the big reveal. As the time came for us to meet, I went to the window and watched vigilantly for the moment she emerged from her apartment building, which was kitty corner to the bar. Finally she began to make her way across the street. From that distance I couldn't really tell how she looked. I quickly shot back into the bar area not wanting to seem desperate. When she entered the bar I stood from my chair about 20 feet away as she approached with a big beautiful smile. She was GORGEOUS!!! My heart was pounding and without hesitation she came right to me and gave me a warm embrace. I believed she was pleased and relieved by what she saw as well. "Nice to finally meet you" I said as I hugged her back. She had these big beautiful brown eyes that instantly put me at ease. We sat and ordered a couple of beers and began talking and just like the 3 phone conversations, it came so natural to us as if we'd known each other for years. We downed the last of our "Summer Shandy's" and decided to head to the game.

The date was June 19th (19 has always been my favorite number) it was a beautiful late spring night just prior to the summer solstice. We got there about an hour before the game so we decided to sit at a beer garden. On our way up to the beer garden all the tables were seemingly taken but I noticed a group of young guys ready to vacate their spot. Just as they were about to leave I overheard one of them saying as they spied Diane making her way towards them, "Oh look at what's heading our way! Check it out! Gorgeous!" Now I tell you this not to brag on Diane who is gorgeous but to let you know that she was oblivious to the whole thing. Diane is so humble that she had no clue they were even checking her out let alone talking about her as she approached. This caught me by surprise and I loved this quality about her. Once the game began we sat about 20 rows behind home plate and although the game was a close one we had barely noticed as we just talked, drank beer, had a hot dog, laughed and truly enjoyed each others company. I simply felt "at home" in her presence.

In the days and weeks that followed, Diane and I just grew closer and closer. It was all very natural and seemed as though it was just meant to be. This is what scared me. I was falling for this woman and I was frightened by how deeply I felt for her. My Divorce was rough and the idea of going down the path of love again truly made me nervous & afraid. Yet every moment I spent with her just felt right. Diane seemed so sure about us that this also gave me pause. Diane had never been married, although her last boyfriend she was with on and off for the last 10 years. She told me that she never felt for him the way she was feeling for me. There was something about the relationship she had with him that just never felt right. She was always afraid to take that "next step" with him. She seemed to have no fear or trepidation when it came to us. I hadn't introduced her to my children yet because I wanted to be sure about our relationship before I took that step. I just didn't know when or how to know if I was "sure" about us. After dating for a couple of months I decided to take her away for a romantic weekend. Spending this time together I felt would give us a better indicator of how strong this relationship was and how truly compatible we were. I chose one of my all time favorite cities: NEW ORLEANS!

Being a speaker means there is a lot of travel involved therefore like Jonny Cash sang, "I've Been Everywhere" and NAWLINS' is a fantastic city! The diverse culture, the food, the architecture and the music are utterly unique and amazing. With the charbroiled oysters at "Dragos" & zydecho music at "Tipitinas" you simply can't go wrong. I really wanted Diane to experience this city and I wanted to see how we would be together on a mini vacation. Needless to say, we were having an incredible time. During our courtship Diane had introduced me to some music she thought I'd like. One artist in particular was Jason Mraz. She knew how much I loved James Taylor and this guy was described as a younger version of him. His biggest hit is a song called "I'm Yours" and he is very good so we would listen to him quite a bit. As luck would have it, he just happened to be putting on a concert in New Orleans the weekend we were there. Diane decided to surprise me and she bought us two "VIP" tickets to see him. On the morning of the 2nd day while enjoying beignets at "Cafe du Monde" she showed me the tickets. I was thrilled and again impressed that she would do this for us. I suggested we go to dinner first then the show but she explained how these VIP tickets included dinner and drinks prior to the show. So that evening we headed to the venue and made our way to the VIP room.

Once in the VIP room you could see why it was called that. It was a beautiful room, more like a lounge with exceptional catered food and any drink you'd like. So Diane and I loaded up our plates, grabbed a drink and felt like "big wigs" as we just hung out with the other "VIP's." After having our fair share of food and drinks we decided to head into the concert. Part of the deal was when we were ready our own personal Usher would escort us to our seats. We told the hostess that we were ready to head into the show and lo and behold an Usher immediately came to our table. We handed her our VIP tickets and followed her into the concert. Once we entered the venue I noticed there was an opening act already performing. We had no idea there even was an opening act. It was some young woman dancing and singing up on stage and I had no clue who she was. The Usher headed to the main middle isle, turned left and started heading toward the stage. We passed the 30th row and kept going. We passed the 20th row and kept going and then passed the 10th row and kept heading toward the stage! I have been to tons of concerts in my life and I had never had seats this good. I was so excited to see how close we would actually be. The Usher just kept going until we reached the front row! We were placed in the first two seats right on the middle aisle directly at the middle of the stage! I looked at Diane and told her, "This is amazing! I've never been in the front row! The opening act was just finishing up a song and again I had no idea who she was. When she finished her song they wheeled out a Grand Piano to the center of the stage and she sat at it directly in front of us. Now, before I continue I need to have you understand what I was feeling at that moment. I am falling in love with Diane but at the same time I am feeling so afraid to put myself out there again and be vulnerable. I had been thru a lot and felt I simply couldn't handle another heartbreak. Then, amidst all those feelings, the young woman on stage sitting at the piano began to play. The moment she hit the first few keys on the piano I recognized the song immediately. It was "A Thousand Years" from the Twilight movie! Those opening notes are immediately recognizable. It was at that moment that I knew who the opening act was, it was Christina Perri!

Then suddenly, everything around me froze and I swear to you, Christina Perri was looking right at me as she sang those magical words about fearing and then ultimately accepting LOVE!

It was as if she was singing exactly what I was feeling. I was in some kind of trance completely immersed in the moment and seeing nothing but Christina Perri singing to me! The very next moment I was broken from the trance because Diane reached over and grabbed my hand and as I turned to look at her, all I could see were her big beautiful eyes staring directly into mine and her radiant and knowing smile at precisely the moment Cristina about a true love that has finally come after a thousand years!

In that moment all the fear I was feeling just left my being. I have never experienced anything like that moment. It felt as though the Universe was telling me something so pure and sure and I couldn't help but feel nothing but this incredible depth of LOVE for Diane. It was a LOVE so real and powerful that I finally recognized in that moment that she was the ONE! The ONE for me and her smile and touch told me that she knew I was the ONE for her! It was one of the most spectacular moments of my life! Then just as Christina Perri finished the song, out of nowhere, a different Usher appeared with another couple standing behind him as he leaned down and said to me, "Sir, these are not your seats. Please follow me." He then proceeded to take us back 43 rows to what we're our actual seats!

Now I realize this story sounds "unbelievable" but I swear to you that is exactly what happened. For one song, THAT SONG, we were put in the front row center and they weren't even our seats! I knew in my heart and without any doubt that that moment was meant to be! That song was meant for us. It was meant for me. It was what I needed to experience to know that what we have is a true and abiding LOVE. It was simply amazing and since that moment I've never felt an ounce of fear or anxiety about my relationship with Diane. All I've felt is a deep and passionate LOVE and we are happier than ever! I know that entire experience was a SIGN!!! I believe that if you are open to it, that you may discover "signs" along your journey in life that are there to point you in the direction you are meant to go. This is possible and can work if we are striving to live an authentic life. When you are being true to yourself you will be more likely to recognize these signs thru events, experiences and people that come into your life. Allow yourself to be open and do your best to live an "honestly" and "authentically" for when you do the answers to life's deeper questions will come.

THE GIFT OF PAIN

People ask me all the time, "How were you able to run a mile in under four minutes?" My answer is, "You need to learn how to practice dealing with pain." They always look confused after I say this and I say it to illicit that very reaction. Because inevitably the next question becomes: "What do you mean?" In every race I have run whether I won or finished in last place the one constant, the one thing all those races have in common is at some point during that race, it's gonna hurt! At a certain point of any distance race, pain begins to set in. Sometimes it comes in an overwhelming rush, other times it is a gradual building. It can start as a whisper of discomfort and eventually becoming a scream of anguish. One thing for sure, no matter how it comes, it always shows up. When it does, it is best to welcome it as an old friend. Like someone that your very familiar with. When one takes this approach with pain and suffering it helps you cope with it in a more effective way. It activates that part of your being that will be proactive about protecting oneself from it. Being prepared for the pain is key but it's only half the battle.

In practice, distance runners use a technique called interval training. This is where you break down a distance into its smaller parts and practice running at a fast pace more comfortably and consistently. For example, the mile is typically broken down into 4 quarter miles. If you want to run a four minute mile then on paper it's simple, learn how to run 4 consecutive 1/4 miles at 60 seconds per quarter. During interval training we may do 10 X 1/4 mile at 60 second pace with 45 seconds of jogging rest in between. This is conditioning our bodies and our minds to run at that exact pace. Inevitably, around the 5th 1/4, the intervals start to hurt. As the pain of each interval increases, one must learn to deal with it while maintaining the pace. Needless to say, it is hard but that's the point. It should be hard. If you keep at it, eventually it becomes easier as your body becomes more fit and conditioned to handle it. It's literally practicing with pain.

Think about the part of your job/career that is the most challenging? What areas of your life do you tend to experience the most discomfort or pain? The key to changing anything that becomes a problem is first being able to acknowledge that you have a problem. This awareness can open the creative portion of your brain to seek solutions. Once you've activated that part of your brain you become empowered to take the steps to fix the problem. What starts to happen is you begin to breakdown what needs to be done in order to create a more desired result. One must be in a calm state of mind to begin to find these solutions. If you find yourself in emotional pain, give yourself time, time to experience the pain while trying to understand its origins. Our emotional pain can distort our perceptions and thinking as it misleads. Let me share an example.

There was a researcher watching three toddlers playing with 3 identical plastic toy boxes that had knobs and buttons on it. One particular red button, when slid to the right would open the top of the box and a cute little puppy would pop out. The first toddler became fixated on the purple button pushing and pulling it to no avail. She could not get the puppy to pop up and she began to cry. The second toddler, a little boy watched as this little girl failed and thus didn't even attempt to release his puppy, he just started crying right along with her. The third toddler, another little girl tried all the buttons and knobs until eventually she figured it out. She discovered that the red button released her puppy. This result had her cheering and laughing.

What's fascinating about this study is the power of the mind over what eventually gets accomplished. If your mind can convince you that you are incapable of something and you believe it, your actions follow that belief and you will begin to feel helpless. This can cause you to stop trying to soon or to never try at all which only makes us more convinced that we cannot succeed. This is why so many people function well under their actual capabilities and potential because somewhere along the way a single failure or a trusted person convinced them that they couldn't succeed and they believed it.

Once someone becomes convinced of something, it is very difficult to change their mind. It is natural to feel demoralized or defeated after you fail but we must not allow ourselves to become convinced that we cannot succeed. We must fight against those feelings that can cause us to give up or become apathetic and persevere against feelings of helplessness. To become disempowered will create an overwhelming sense of failure and pain. We need to break this negative cycle before it begins.

Sometimes our minds and our feelings don't always act as the "trust worthy friends" that we think they should be. Instead, they can be that really moody friend that can be totally trustworthy and supportive one minute and really nasty and critical the next. Our sense of self, our self-esteem is so critical as to how we experience our world from the inside out. There have been dozens of studies that clearly show that when we have poor self esteem, we actually become more vulnerable to stress and anxiety thus, causing failures and rejections to hurt much more. If we don't have the tools to deal with emotional pain then we literally become held hostage by the myriad of things that can go wrong in life. This can unleash the kind of pain that can destroy us. We need to break it down and understand the roots of the pain so that we may better understand its presence in our lives. When we understand the roots of its presence we can begin to learn how to let it go. We need to build resiliency. We need to accept that pain at times will be part of our experience but it doesn't have to take up permanent residence in our hearts, minds and souls.

TO BE RESILIENT

One very important trait we must learn to develop is RESILIENCY. In dealing with the PAIN of our lives, becoming resilient is key. Building resiliency is all about "doing." What is great about this is the knowing that we have the ability to develop and learn how to become resilient. It is a learned trait. I do believe that our genetic code plays a part, but only a part. Are some people naturally more resilient then others? Absolutely. But I believe that it only makes up part of the equation. The rest can and certainly is developed over time. There are certain components in building resilience. One discovers this when they suffer. When life delivers a "body blow" or "gut punch" and you find yourself way out of your comfort zone. This is when you become tested in having to discover your true inner strength. I know for a fact that being a distance runner most of my life requires endurance and that word comes from the root "endure" which means to suffer patiently. Think about what that means, "to suffer patiently." You realize to finish this workout or this race I'm going to have to deal with the pain and the hurt. In the end, you come to realize, I can do this. I can get thru this. I can ENDURE this. That is where the resilience begins to develop. It's much like courage. Courage is not the lack of fear, rather it is the presence of fear but you do what you need to do and face it. That is where the courage is created.

THE STORY OF EPICTETUS

Epictetus (whose name translates as The Acquired One) was born to a slave woman and spent the first 30 years of his life as a slave much of it in chains. As a child he was bought by an extremely violent and depraved man who once twisted Epictetus' leg so bad that as he did so Epictetus warned him, "You are going to break my leg" and eventually when it snapped, Epictetus looked his owner in the eye and said, "I told you that would happen." From this, his leg was shattered and he walked with a limp for the rest of his life. Not long after, he began to attend the lectures of stoic philosophers and was fascinated by the philosophy. When he was finally freed from slavery in his thirties, Epictetus decided to become a Philosophy teacher. He was an amazing lecturer and it wasn't long before he gained quite a following from people of all walks of life. His primary focus that built such a following was the subject of resiliency.

Epictetus was a brilliant source on this subject because of the life he had lived. He was the epitome of RESILIENCE and he called it a skill. He taught his students that this skill will help us lead an untroubled life. This skill will help us overcome the darkest of circumstances. He knew how to teach it because he had mastered it thru his own experience and thru his own life. He called it, "discovering the power of ENDURANCE." The first and most important key is the understanding of what is up to us and what is not up to us. In other words, recognizing what we can control compared to what we cannot. Those that understand this distinction realize the vital difference between those that live with resilience from those that don't. For example, Epictetus liked to use the example of those who insult us. What other people say is not up to us but how we respond is. So if someone succeeds in provoking you, he said you must realize that your mind is complicit in the provocation. He called this the "faculty of choice" and he claimed, "This is our greatest power, our most efficacious gift and our uniquely human capability." This realization was critical to his own resilience and survival as a slave.

When life hits us hard and fate deals us a bad hand, we always retain the power to choose our response, our attitude, our perspective, our judgments and opinions. This ideology and philosophy was very empowering. It gave people a real sense of personal strength and that instilled hope. Epictetus went on to say that every event has two handles: One by which it can be carried and one by which it can't. If your Brother does you wrong, he said don't grab it by his wronging because this is the handle incapable of lifting it. Instead use the other, that he is your Brother and that you were raised together and then you will have hold of the handle that carries. When adversity hits, the question becomes, "Which handle will we grab?" Will we grab the one of resentment, of bitterness, of anger and of unfairness or the one of forgiveness, of strength, of fortitude, of looking for the good, of looking for what we might do with what has happened? Are we going to grasp the problem or the opportunity? There is almost always some good hiding within or around the bad. You have to look for it and you have to grab hold of it. This is how we thrive in life. One must also come to the realization that sometimes there isn't anything we can do. Sometimes it is not up to us and all you can do is let go and move on. This is what Epictetus called: "The Art Of Acquiescence." This is a surrendering to fate and accepting that there is a larger plan. This is a bold optimism infused with determination. This is the recognition that there is something's we cannot see and something higher than ourselves. This way of thinking and believing makes us more powerful and more unstoppable in every human way. Epictetus was able to see that the adversity and difficulty that he went thru was shaping the man he was to become giving him the ability to instruct others in a way that would resonate. It came from his experience and from his heart and soul. It was authentic and that's why so many were so inspired by him!

Accepting the pain and suffering that comes with life is not easy to do. Epictetus said, "We must go into a hard winters training and not rush into things for which we haven't prepared." This is where you get the love of challenges, of the embracing of adversity because we know there will be a payoff in the end. We will develop endurance and resilience and this will completely enhance the quality of our lives. The pain and struggle will be the training for what the World will throw at us. This takes work and thus when talking about resilience we must realize it must be something we are willing to build. As we construct it more and more in our lives we become more powerful and stronger as we continue our journey. It takes practice and preparation and that comes from the suffering itself. So every time life throws something at you, realize that this is your training, a chance to get better. When this becomes your perspective of pain, it will empower you, embolden you and your resilience will build. Epictetus promised, "In time you will come to realize there is nothing that you don't have the means to tolerate." Turn what you have to do into what you get to do! Turn what life throws at you into the fuel to the fire that is making you strong, courageous and RESILIENT!

To be "resilient" means the capacity to recover from adversity. The nature of things tells us that life will be difficult at times. We cannot change this but we can prepare for it. That is the key to Peak Performance and living our out our true potential: PREPARATION! So lets talk a little bit more deeply on how to cultivate & develop resilience. I've said a few times in this book and I say it at practically every presentation I give that: "Self Awareness is the Key to Transformation." This is particularly important when working to develop resilience. We need to get an understanding of our perspective and the role it plays in the experience of our lives. Becoming aware of the way we choose to see our world, where we place our focus is vital building resilience. Here's an example of what I mean.

CONSCIOUSNESS

 Back when I was training for the Olympic trials, I had gone to a seminar to learn more about race strategy and building confidence in my performance. During this seminar the presenter, who was a sports psychologist said he was going to ask us 3 questions. He instructed us that if we were to answer: "YES" to any of the 3 questions, we should not say the word "YES" but rather just stand up. Standing up means "YES." If you want to respond "NO" then don't say "NO" just stay seated. Staying seated will mean "NO." He continued, "Ok, here we go. Question # 1, how many people in here can sing?" In that moment a bunch of thoughts fired off in my brain about my singing. What I mainly remember hearing in my thoughts was all the negative feedback I've heard in my life regarding my singing. In fact, the first thing that came to mind were the words "You suck at singing!" Thus, I stayed in my seat. I did not get up. In fact, only about 10% of the room was actually standing.

 "Question #2: How many people in here can draw?" When I heard this question my mind went blank. I've never really gotten into art and drawing was something that I never did so I just sat there, as did 80% of the audience.

 Question #3, "How many people in here can dance?" Instantly I heard a voice in my head say "GET UP" so I sprang to my feet and stood proudly along with about 10% of the audience. Why did I stand so quickly? Throughout my life I have always had people say to me what a great dancer I was. In junior high my impersonation of John Travolta from Saturday Night Fever was spot on. In High School it was Michael Jackson. I always had natural rhythm and people noticed and loved when I danced. The feedback was always positive therefore, I stood up!.

When he finished his 3 questions he then said, "Now did I ask if you could do either of these 3 things WELL or GOOD?" Then it hit me. He wasn't asking if I thought I was good at this, he asked am I capable of doing this. I obviously did not clearly hear what he was asking. What I heard is my interpretation of what he was asking. This miscommunication was entirely my doing. It was very revelatory how my actions followed my belief that I've embraced when it came to my singing, drawing and dancing. You see if we only hear the negative self- talk we have within then our beliefs and actions will follow to create negative outcomes. If we hear within that "I'm not good enough" and come to believe it, then what will happen next is self sabotage or a self fulfilling prophecy. I will begin to make the choices and take the actions that will back up the belief that I am not good enough. Most of the time, I'm not even aware of what I'm doing. This clearly illustrates that sometime's our pain is unconsciously self-inflicted.

This is why being mindful and aware are key to positive mental health. When we live a "conscious" life it will help us live authentically. This will give us perspective and that is why each of us need to take a self reflective inward journey to discover why we think and believe the things we do. The key to that journey is to discover if there is any truth to the beliefs we have especially the ones we have about ourselves. In other words, is my limiting belief valid or was it someone else's insecurities projected onto me? As we begin to become "aware" we begin to build our resiliency.

PROJECTION

Let's take a look at this term called "Projection."

Projection: Unconsciously taking unwanted emotions or traits you don't like about yourself and attributing them to someone else.

I have discovered that the older I get the more aware I have become of the projection going on all around me. It is a very difficult thing to strive to live an emotionally healthy life. To do so you need to take accountability for your thoughts, feelings and actions. In other words, you need to "OWN" your stuff. When people are not willing to do this, they inevitably project these negative feelings, insecurities, fears and beliefs on those around them. This is why being a parent is one of the hardest endeavors you will ever undertake. It is very easy to pass all your negative unconscious beliefs onto your children. This is how we are able to explain multi generational hatred, racism and bigotry. I will never believe a child comes into the world with "HATE" in their heart. The hate that they embrace was passed down to them from their parents or those entrusted to care for them. Now imagine the emotional pain that stems from that hate being directed at oneself. (It's not hard for many to imagine because it is their reality.) If the only message you hear from those who are supposed to LOVE you is that you are no good and worthless then it's highly likely that you will adopt that belief about yourself. When that happens, you will treat yourself with contempt. Your actions will follow that belief and it will become evident in your behavior. What is so sad about this is that there is literally no truth to it. It is in fact a projection of how the one delivering that message actually feels about themselves. The more you become aware of this the more you are able to see it for what it really is. You can then choose not to believe any of it because in reality it has nothing to do with you.

One of the first things we need to ask ourselves when confronted with an obstacle to our own success is, "What is it that's holding me back?" When we have conflict in our lives, especially internal conflict we first must take a good look at it in order to understand its roots. Am I the one creating the conflict? Is this conflict something that is true or have I manufactured it? If I attach or bind myself to what is negative or unsatisfactory in my life then how could I ever feel satisfied? Yet we tend to do this to ourselves much of the time. Once you discover what you are doing that causes pain and discontent in your life ask yourself, "What will I do about it?" Notice I said "Will" instead of "Can" because "Will" means some form of action and "Can" means some sort of understanding. We always need to be looking to ignite our passion so as to drive thru any obstacle that is external and let go of any obstacle that is within. This doesn't mean that you won't experience some pain or hardship along the way. That pain and hardship in my opinion are part of the process. It is the chance for you to define in your heart and mind how bad you really want something. In other words, what are you going to do about it?

It seems as though our world is set up in a way to try and make us feel discontent. This discontent is the fuel that keeps us wanting. It's the feeling that at times makes us believe we are not good enough the way we are and thus we must change ourselves or our circumstance. Sometimes the things holding us back are the thoughts and beliefs we have about a particular obstacle. If we believe the obstacle is just to big then we will lose our incentive and drive to do anything about it. This is the moment you discover if you are truly committed to your own happiness and to your own fulfillment. It's your Passion & Drive fueled by your belief that no obstacle is too big to overcome! It is your humility that will inform you that you have been the cause of much of your own pain. How you choose to practice or live your life on a daily basis will become your experience.

(Just a thought) "I'm very confounded by why we as human beings tend to be so hard on ourselves? I have no idea where that comes from yet when I talk to people from all over the world, it seems to be the norm. Far to often I am my own worst enemy. Maybe it's because we literally can't escape ourselves. I mean we are always with ourselves and even the best of friends or happiest of couples have their issues and people do get on each other's nerves. Therefore, it would make sense that the relationship you have with yourself is key to the overall experience of your life. So I guess the thing to look into is the intricacies of the relationship we have with self."

A state of "well-being" comes down to our mind and its awareness. Like an athlete trains his or her body to be fit, our minds need training too. Mind training is grounded in the idea and understanding that two opposite mental factors cannot happen at the same time. You can go from Love to Hate but you cannot experience both at the same time towards the same object or the same person. Therefore, a natural cure to the emotions that are destructive to our inner "well-being" is the fact that it cannot last or take up residence in my awareness unless I allow it.

All emotions are fleeting and the only way it can linger is because of the focus and awareness we choose to give it. Each time our minds go to the emotions that cause us pain it reinforces the emotions power and annoyance it has over us. It becomes a self-perpetuating process that if we do not become aware of our will create our life's experience. To begin a new process and awareness, instead of looking outward we need to look inward. We need to look into the depth of who we are. On the surface of our minds where a negative thought and emotion can arise we have the choice not need to attach our focus to it. For example, think of a time in your life when someone mistreated you. If we dwell on the thought and pay mind to it then it will create the emotion of hurt & anger itself and the body quickly follows suit with tension and stress thus creating a physical experience of the emotion. We are now not just having feelings of anger, we are angry. What if, as the initial thought arises of the mistreatment that caused us hurt and anger we choose not to give it our awareness? What happens then? (Remember Epictetus and what we control) I believe the thought will move along like the clouds passing overhead in the sky and our awareness might now be on the sun that was behind the clouds giving us warmth. We are now in a whole new experience. This training of the mind is not simple. Just like running a sub Four-minute mile was not simple. It took years of training. It took us years to develop the way in which our minds work so it will take time to experience a new way. Once we commit to change then the training itself can produce an awareness and experience of something new. This will empower us to continue along the journey toward a more positive experience of our life. This mind transformation takes daily practice. This is why so many people are discovering meditation although its been around for thousands of years. Meditation is mind transformation.

In recent years scientists and researchers have made great strides in the area of brain plasticity. It used to be believed that by the time you reach adulthood that your brain was about as developed as it could get. It was believed that any changes in the brain once we hit adulthood are insignificant. We now know this is not true at all. The brain has incredible plasticity. This means its potential to change and adapt at any stage of life is not only possible but rather quite probable. In order for such changes to take place requires significant practice. The training of the mind needs to be a daily, ongoing and consistent endeavor. A few years back a comprehensive study was done on Buddhist monks from various parts of the world who were considered experts in the practice of meditation. They placed them in an MRI for 3 1/2 hours as they meditated to observe the activity of the brain. What they found was that they were able to significantly increase the activity in the left side of the pre frontal cortex. In fact, in some cases the activity in this part of the brain was off the charts. Why is this significant? This was significant because that is the side where the experience and feelings of compassion and love and happiness are formulated and experienced! This proved to the researchers that mind training not only works, it matters. What I believe to be most significant about this is when we practice mind training and we work on meditation, it increases our experience of love & compassion. This inspires us to share that love & compassion with the world around us. Therefore, meditation is not only good for us it is good for the world at large.

MEDITATION

One thing that became quickly apparent was I needed to learn to quiet my mind. I had made the connection that there were times my obsessive thinking could take over and completely affect my mood and my behavior. I had to become friends with silence. This is a tall order for me, for God sake I speak for a living! The kind of silence I needed was not just from my mouth but rather, from my mind. I needed to begin with the act of being silent, literally being silent. I've heard it suggested that we should set aside two times a day for silence. So I did. The following are my notes after the first time I sat alone in total silence for 17 minutes.

-Okay, I just finished my first attempt at silent meditation and although the room and outside environment was very quiet my mind was anything but. I simply could not quiet my mind. It made me feel agitated and exhausted. I kept hearing that "coach" in my head telling me to focus! That voice in my head kept pleading for me to quiet my mind and yet that voice was the one thing that was in the way. I'd find myself thinking about what I had to get done then I'd redirect my mind to try to be quiet. It felt like a futile experience. I am frustrated but at least I tried. I realized that within our minds we have conflicts going on all the time. Sometimes its a conflict of priorities, for instance what will I do next? When it comes to the people in my life we become conflicted with who will I spend my time with and how much? And finally the inner conflict of who we truly are to who we have pretend to be. I've realized thru a single meditative attempt that all these conflicts going on at once create such a noisy mind and thus an anxiety filled reality.

This was just my first go at it. I will try again tomorrow.

So the next day I tried again:

-Today was better. Once the meditation began I immediately fell back into my over active mind but this time I decided not to pay attention to it. I remember as a kid I used to daydream all the time during class. The teacher would be talking and I'd be lost in my daydream. I just wasn't paying any attention to her. This is what I did with the noise in my head and before long I began to feel detached and peaceful. It didn't last long but I found myself there for about 15 minutes. I suppose the real understanding will come when I don't acknowledge time at all. I will keep trying.

This was an opening of understanding things a little more deeply. Legend has it that the Buddha once gave a "silent sermon" in which he held up a flower and gazed at it. He did this for quite awhile to a room full of onlookers who seemed to stand there, not knowing what was happening. One of the spectators, a monk named Mahakasyapa began to smile. He is said to be the only one in the audience to understand the sermon. That smile later became the origins of ZEN. A peaceful enlightenment or understanding is something that I knew could be so beneficial in my life right now.

I remember watching the movie Phenomenon and John Travolta's character George Malley was highly stressed and could not calm his racing overactive mind as he frenetically worked in his garden. Just then the wind picked up and blew through the great live oaks he had in his front yard. He suddenly stopped what he was doing, looked up at the tree and in a state of "Zen" or enlightenment seemed to become one with that tree. He stood swaying with the branches and the leaves as though he was an extension of them and just calmly and effortlessly was totally in sync and in the moment of just being with that tree. For me, that seems to capture what the Buddha must have been trying to convey in his silent sermon. It is the essence of what I'd like to attain in my life. It would be wonderful to have a place I could go for an experience of peace. Imagine how wonderful it could be to not have to go on vacation to a beach, or to climb a mountain or walk in the woods to create it. What if I could get there no matter where I was because that place dwelled within me? Hindu's call this enlightenment, Buddhists say its "Nirvana," and the Christians call it salvation. Think about it for a second, no matter who we are or where we come from we are all universally seeking this. It is an experience! Sometimes we get to "caught up" in trying to define the meaning of life when really what were after is an experience of feeling truly ALIVE!

(THE FLOWER MEDITATION)

I decided to try a meditation with a flower. I felt that focusing on something might be a more effective way to a meditative state. So I went and bought my favorite one, the Sun Flower. Here's what happened: I sat in my bedroom in total silence with all the lights off except one that was shining directly on the flower. As I stared deeply at the flower the first thing that came to me was the sheer radiance of it. It was stunning and alive to me. Then without warning the word sunshine came into my mind. I began to see the brilliance of the sun in that flower. I then heard a quiet voice deep within and it began singing to me.

"You are my sunshine, my only sunshine. You make me happy when skies are grey. You'll never know dear how much I love you, please don't take my sunshine away."

I then closed my eyes and was brought back to my son's bed when he was about 2 years old and I would sing that to him before he fell asleep. Then I saw my daughters beautiful brown eyes looking up at me when she was just a baby and I was singing that to her. It was the line, "you'll never know dear how much I love you" that kept playing in my mind. I was then deep in an experience of gratitude thinking of all those I love so dearly in my life. I could see their faces so clearly it was like they were right there with me. I was just smiling feeling so immersed in a feeling of love and warmth as if the sun was shining directly upon me. I lingered there for a while until the line from the song, "please don't take my sunshine away" came into my mind. My consciousness then shifted to the loved ones I have lost. I began recalling moments with them. Beautiful moments that have forever marked the journey of my life and again I was feeling such gratitude. I could experience them again within me and I felt love.

After about 20 minutes or so my eyes opened and the flower was their staring back at me. I came back to the conscious moment of the radiance, brilliance and warmth of that flower. This time, thru this meditation, I went somewhere. I had gone to a place deep within where wonderful moments of my journey are still alive. I realized right then and there it was a place I could go when I needed. It was beautiful! I liked this meditation...I liked it a lot.

~"No man steps into the same river twice, for its not the same river and he's not the same man" ~Hericlitus

The abundance of the relationship we have with ourselves lives in the subconscious mind. It is believed that the conscious thoughts we have each and every day, the things we choose to focus on is what feeds the subconscious mind. Therefore, we can improve our relationship with ourselves by what we feed our subconscious. This takes a deep concentration on what we consciously focus on. Become aware and mindful of the way you "see" and the way you "feel" about you. What is your perspective? What do you believe about you? What is the story you tell about you? This is a direct reflection of the identity you have chosen for and that identity is the basis of your experience of life. Our subconscious mind plays a vital role in the existence of identity. We have the ability to program the subconscious mind through our conscious thoughts, imaginations & intentions. Throughout each day and especially at night, take time to say, visualize and feel positive affirmations. For example, one I use is "I AM LOVE...I AM LOVED...I LOVE." In all of these three sayings I see myself as love, as being loved and as loving others...including myself. In this I have the experience of knowing that what I say see and feel are true. Let me tell you how I came to this.

One of the most beautiful examples I have of a person who personified LOVE is my Aunt Peggy. We grew close when I was very young. My

Mom had a nervous breakdown when I was three. The day that happened is the earliest conscious memory I have in my life. Due to severe panic attacks, my Mom became an agoraphobic. That's a person deathly afraid of leaving the home because of the panic attack that could happen while out in the world. It had happened before and my Mother became paralyzed by the fear of it happening again. Therefore, my Mom would not, under any circumstance leave the home and on many days she wouldn't leave her bedroom. I was 3 years old when this all began and it lasted for 3 years. I have two older sisters who were 5 & 7 at the time and we needed help. One of the people who came to help was my Moms younger sister Peggy. She cared for us during a good part of that time and I believe now that is where our strong bond was created. My Aunt was a ray of sunshine to all who knew her. She had an amazing story. She was a Dominican Nun in the Catholic faith for 25 years. She then fell in love with a Priest and they both had to leave the Church to become married. She went on to become the Principal at a Catholic middle school in a suburb outside of Chicago. She was beloved by students and staff. This came as no surprise because she was beloved by all who knew her. It was her loving way and her optimism and enthusiasm for life that people were attracted to. She was truly "one of a kind" and I loved her dearly. When she was 53 years old she felt a sharp pain in her back. She thought she had probably wrenched it in someway and just ignored the pain. One day the pain became so severe she decided to go to the doctor to see what was wrong. When the X-rays came back, she was diagnosed with stage four Bone Cancer and was given about a year left to live. Bone cancer is one of the most painful cancers there is and the suffering is immense. When we heard this diagnosis it was heart breaking. Talk about someone who didn't deserve such a fate but I learned from this that "deserve" has got nothing to do with it. It's also why I have a problem with those who believe that "Everything happens for a reason" as if there is some great lesson to be learned from such news. (For example, what is the reason that millions of people, many being children are liter- ally starving to death in our World today? I can't see any "reason" or silver lining to be found... but I digress.) Needless to say her final year was a very painful one. She went thru quite a depression during most of that year until at some point she had come to acceptance.

She wouldn't see many people during that final year but one of the people she would see was me. I'll never forget the last time I saw her. When I walked into the home she and her husband had, there she was lying in a hospital bed right in the middle of the family room. They had set her up there the last few months because her bones had become so brittle that she couldn't get around anymore without the risk of breaking those bones. She was very weak, she had lost a significant amount of weight and she had an oxygen mask on her face. When she saw me come into the room her eyes lit up (like they always had when she saw me) which always made me feel so good...so loved. I sat beside her and held her hand and talked to her while choking back the tears with every ounce of strength I had. Her husband was telling stories about some of the adventures they had shared when he revealed something none of us knew. They would go to Las Vegas like 4 times a year! We had no idea that our Aunt Peggy loved to play the slots. We also learned that she didn't just play, she'd win! Peggy's husband Paul told a story in how he couldn't win at slots to save his life. On one particular trip she had won close to $2000.00 yet he on the other hand lost $500. As my Uncle Paul very frustratingly continued to play on and pull the one armed bandit he just couldn't hit a thing. Then he said, "Peggy walked up and asked hows it going?" Paul replied in a defeated tone, "not well." So my Aunt Peggy said, "Let me give her a try." She proceeded to put the lever and hit a jackpot of another $1000! As my Uncle Paul told the story, he was laughing and regaling in the good fortune his wife had. Peggy then pulled the oxygen mask off her face, turned to me and in a very strained and tired voice said, "I've always been very lucky."

I couldn't believe she just said that. She is lying there in pain, literally on her deathbed being ravaged by a cruel and so undeserved disease at a relatively young age and all she can talk about is how lucky she has been. How does one become so utterly lovely like that? I have discovered that it's a choice. It is a choice in how to see ones life. It is a choice to be grateful instead of cynical. It is a choice to see beauty and light in all things and not darkness and decay. I also realized that this choice is one we can all make yet so few do. My Aunt Peggy strived to make that choice each day of her life. Because of that choice the differences she made in all the lives she touched was transformational and profound. Peggy had always been this way so why did I expect her to be any different now? I don't know but I did. Don't get me wrong, for I'm sure she had her bad days. I'm sure she had her moments of doubt and pain and I wonder if she ever asked, "Why me?" I honestly don't know but I can tell you I never heard it or saw her without a complete faith that sustained her through it all. It was a faith that inspired those lucky enough to know her.

As the stories continued from Uncle Paul I sat beside her and just held tightly to her hand. We laughed and smiled and it was beautiful. I then began to tell her about some new stories about my kids. My son Jack at the time was 3 years old and my daughter Gracie was just one. As I waxed on about Jacks latest feat or Gracie's first word, something became clear to me and then suddenly the tears just started welling in my eyes and silently falling down my cheeks. Peggy said in a muffled voice due to oxygen mask covering her mouth, "Oh honey, what's wrong?" What had hit me so hard was the fact that my children would not know this spectacular human being lying here before me and it made me profoundly Sad. I composed myself and said, "I am so sad that my children will not know you." She then did the best she could to raise her head from the pillow and with a very frail hand she removed the oxygen mask from her face and looked me directly in the eyes and said, "Oh Eddie they will know me... they will always know me thru you." She then smiled, laid her head down and placed the oxygen mask back over her mouth. My heart swelled, the tears continued to just roll down my cheeks as I kissed her on the forehead and whispered, "I Just Love You So." That was the last time I saw her. Two days later she was gone.

A few days after she passed a package arrived from Peggy's husband Paul addressed to me. It was a beautiful picture of Peggy with a note that said, "Peggy wanted you to have this Eddie. She loved you with all her heart and soul and she was so proud of you. Before she passed she requested that you please do the Eulogy at her funeral mass." When I got this picture I knew I wanted to place it somewhere prominent but I didn't know where. My wife and I had just converted our dining room into a study with brand new bookshelves. We had just finished filling the shelves with all our books and the only shelf available was the bottom shelf of the first bookshelf as you enter the room. For the time being I just decided to place it down there until I could figure out where I wanted it to go. Later that evening I was sitting in our new recliner in our new converted sitting room working on the Eulogy when my three year old Son, Jack came running into the room. He abruptly stopped and began staring at the picture of Peggy in the bottom shelf, which happened to be eye level for him. He then proceeded to stand there and silently stare at the picture. I was watching, unbeknownst to him when he then pointed his finger at the Picture and said, "Dada." He then pointed over to me, smiled and said "Dada." He then pointed back to the Picture of Peggy and again said, "Dada." He then did something I will never forget. He leaned in, kissed the picture of Peggy and ran out of the room.

I was sitting there in disbelief of what I just witnessed. Now you need to understand something, Peggy and I do not look alike at all but for whatever reason, when my Son saw her, he also saw me. Then Peggy's words came to me from the last time I saw her: "Eddie, they will always know me thru you." My son saw me in Peggy. I realized in that moment the importance of keeping her alive in me. Her beauty, her compassion and her love are alive in me and thus thru my beauty, my compassion and my love I reveal her to my children.

Later that night I was in bed trying to fall asleep. It was one of those nights where my mind was racing and I was restless and could not doze off. Finally, with the alarm clock ticking away next to my bedside, I began to fade into a deep sleep. It didn't take long before my sub conscious was taking over as I began to dream. I dreamt that I was a reporter waiting for a very important interview. I had no idea who I was to interview. I was sitting in a very small room that was more like a walk in closet. It was a dark and sparse room with only two folding chairs in it. I was seated in one of the chairs with the other chair directly across from me, facing me but empty. As I patiently waited silently in my chair, I heard a thunderous crash and my little room began to shake. Right then, the roof flew off of the tiny room and a bright light began to shine down directly on the chair facing me. Then in a flash, my Aunt Peggy appeared in the chair smiling at me. I couldn't believe it! I said, "Oh my God! Aunt Peggy its you!" She continued to smile her beautiful reassuring smile and said, "I heard you were looking for an interview." Still in shock I replied, "Yes! It would be my honor to interview you for you are one of the best human beings I have ever known!" She said, "Okay then. What would you like to know?" I sat quiet for a moment and then I asked: "You have always been someone I have truly admired and I have looked up to you my whole life. You lived an extraordinary life and everyone who knew you loved you so I guess my first question would be, what is the secret to living such an amazing life?" Peggy smiled a knowing smile and said, "There is no secret for the answers lie within each and everyone of us. We are each beautiful and unique. Therefore, you have to just be YOU! Authentic, honest and open because there is no one else exactly like you. We have to trust in this and have faith that the answers to life's important questions will come. I will say this, your life is the most important gift you will ever receive and it must be treated as so. Life is also an amazing adventure! There is beauty, magic and wonder all around you and within you. The key to living the life you are meant to live is done by connecting to that beauty, magic & wonder and learn to bring it out to share with the world. It is your unique gift to give. We each need to realize that because of our uniqueness what we have to contribute can only come from us. That understanding gives you and your life deep meaning and purpose."

I sat quiet for a moment and took in her words. Then I said, "Now that I'm a parent, I know I'll never be or do anything more important in my life. What should I teach my children so that they can live extraordinary lives?" Peggy reached out her hands and grabbed mine and looked directly into my eyes and said, "Show them that they are loved by loving them completely and unconditionally. Show them that they are stronger and more resilient then they realize and when life knocks them down and they suffer, which at times they will, show them how important it is to ask for help. For when they do they will recognize that there will always be some-one there to help navigate them thru the difficult moments in life. Show them the importance of forgiveness and not just the forgiveness we need to give to others who hurt us but the forgiveness we must learn to give to ourselves. Finally, show them that they are beautiful."

Then suddenly she was gone and that bright light that was shining upon her was now shining on me. I then heard her voice whisper in my ear, "And remember Eddie that you are loved..." At that moment I was awoken by the sound of my Son Jack crying in his room. Jack was 4 years old at the time. I immediately shot out of bed and quickly made my way to his bedroom. "What's the matter buddy? Are you ok?" I said as I sat next to him on his bed rubbing his head while drying his tears. "Dada, I had a bad dream." I reassured him and said, "Oh that happens sometimes but it was just a dream...your ok...I'm here." Jack stopped crying and I hugged him and kissed his forehead. "Go back to sleep son, if you need me just call for me"

As I made my way out of his room I heard my Son say, "I love you Dada" I stopped at the door, looked back, smiled and said "I love you too buddy...Goodnight." And as I laid back in bed I heard my Aunt Peggy's words echo in my mind, "Remember Eddie, you are loved." In that moment I knew she was with me and always will be. I also knew, she was with my children. I came to know that as I go thru pain and suffering at times in my life that it's the people who love me who will help me thru it. It's the love I share with those who truly know and understand my heart and my soul that will support me and carry me along the way when I need it. For in the end, I'd imagine that when you look back on your life, one doesn't think about that great car or house or any material possession they've had in their lives. I believe we think about the people, the relationships that have helped shape who we are. I believe it's the love we not only remember but actually take with us. It's the love that has made the journey so worthwhile. So today, think of those you love and share with them what it is you are feeling and experiencing. Let them know that you carry them in your heart. It WILL BE a magnificent moment and an experience that could change someone's life today...starting with yours. Yes, you will experience pain and suffering but remember it is all part of the process. It wakes you up to the things you truly want and need and love in your world. It helps release your true passion and it ignites action! So remember that there is beauty, magic and wonder all around you and more importantly within you. Connect with it, bring it forth and share it with our world. It is your gift to give and remember to LOVE deeply and passionately along the way for LOVE is not just the destination...it is the journey.

As you can see I believe it is our relationships that are the most important part of our lives and we need to take care to nurture those relationships. For it is thru our relationships that we experience the deepest emotions, connections and experiences we will ever have. My relationship with my Aunt Peggy is one that I cherish with all my heart and she is a part of me. When I find myself being compassionate in the face of hurt, when I find myself being peaceful and calm in the face of turmoil, when I find myself being loving in the face of hate I know that my Aunt Peggy is so very present in me in those moments. She has always and continues to be a presence in the better versions of who I am. For although I know we are unique, we are also a combination of the many people who have a major influence on us as we grow up. It is important to look back and discover who those people are and the impact they've had on your life. When you do you will undoubtedly recognize that they are part of the fabric of you. My courage and resilience is my Mother. My discipline and passion is my

Father. My three siblings are a significant fabric of my being. My teachers, coaches and friends along the journey of life reside within me as well. Every significant relationship we have plays a role in who we are and who we will become.

Inevitably the pain becomes part of the journey. The blood, sweat & tears are the very things that pave the way to your ultimate accomplishments. In fact, I don't believe anything worthwhile happens without it. This is why we need to have passion & drive behind what we are trying to create because it is not going to be easy. It is going to hurt at times. That hurt & pain becomes your test to see how badly you truly want what you say you want. One of my favorite movie quotes is from THE UNTOUCHABLES when Jimmy Malone, who had literally given his life to capture Al Capone, questioned Elliott Ness with his final breath, "What are you prepared to do?" When you know you are willing to deal with the pain that comes with the quest then you know that you are ready to do whatever it takes! The key is knowing in your heart that the pain and the suffering will pass. You will not stay stuck there for it is just a part of life. Your pain is not all there is to who you are. You are so much more than that and life never stays stagnant. Life keeps moving so know that no matter what pain you may encounter in your life, you will not be stuck there. You and your life will keep moving and time will see you thru. Two things you must have are faith and a good solid support network. Take some time and meditate on the people you know you can count on no matter what. When you identify who those people are, let them know what they mean to you. Share with them the your Love & Gratitude that you feel for having them in your life.

I would like to leave you as we end step #5 "WHAT TO DO WHEN THE PAIN HITS" with a simple yet profound poem by Rainier Maria Rilke:

"Let everything happen to you

Beauty and Terror

Just Keep Going

No Feeling is Final"

STEP #6

Set your Destination Point

One of the most important aspects to accomplishing something in life is deciding when you plan on getting it done. Setting a "deadline" or what I like to call a "Destination Point" is crucial. Achieving what you want in life is almost impossible until you set the date you plan to have it done. Setting this point of completion will help you take control over what needs to be done. It helps focus the mind on the finish line, which will empower you to keep moving forward. There is no way to measure your progress without a destination point. Having a destination point will cause you more often than not to commit to what you say you are setting out to do. It makes you accountable! Accountability is key to your personal empowerment.

To help you set the proper "Destination Point" you'll need to take some time to reflect and meditate on it. Allow yourself to visualize what things will look and feel like when you've reached the finish line. Try and become familiar with it in your mind so that you not only believe it is inevitable but a knowing of when it will be real. This gives you an idea of how long you think you will need. For example, in writing this book I struggled with when I would have it completed. It started as an idea 10m years ago and I began to write it slowly as I became more aware of what I wanted this book to be about. I wanted my journey and the wisdom I had gained along the way to be sprinkled within the book therefore, I had no destination point for it. Like myself, it was a work in progress. When the book began to reveal itself to me and I knew specifically what I wanted to say, then I knew it was time to finish it. One day I sat quietly in my room and began to meditate and visualize a good date to have this done. Then it hit me! I decided on the May 6th, 2021 because that was the anniversary of the very first sub 4 Minute Mile run by Dr. Roger Bannister in 1954. I then had the cover of the book created before the book was complete to motivate me to get it done. It was amazing to me how that one decision, to set that date, truly motivated me to finish the book. I believe that once the destination point was created, my Brain became ultra focused on the daily things that needed to happen to make it so. Let me give you an example of a time having the Destination Point set in my game plan truly helped me reach what I had set out to do.

THE GOAL: MAKING THE OLYMPIC TRIALS

Before every Olympiad United States runners are given one year in which to achieve the "qualifying standard" for their events in any track meet officially sanctioned by the Athletics Congress of the USA. Every runner who meets the standard is invited to compete at the trials for a spot on the United States Olympic team. The standard in the 1500 meters (the metric mile) was 3:41.80. That is what I had to run to achieve my long goal of making it to the trials. My personal Best was 3:42.10 so I knew I'd have to run faster then I'd ever had to achieve my goal. It was July, 1992 and I had about a year to do this. The trials were to be held from June 19th thru the 28th in New Orleans, Louisiana. My ultimate goal was to make the Olympic Team but in order to do that you first have to qualify for the Trials. My Coach and I sat down and began to devise the game plan to make this happen. Most of the serious intense work wouldn't begin until we hit indoor track season during the winter but for now we needed to focus on building a strong base until then. That meant the next few months would be high mileage and long endurance runs. We had a few cross country races set up for me to race in but the focus would not be on performing at my highest levels but rather to build toward a much bigger plan. Therefore, we created a calendar thru the fall and set mileage goals along the way designed to build strength. Once we hit December, we would revisit the plan and begin to navigate what would need to be done to qualify for the Olympic trials.

That winter, my Coach and I sat down and laid out the plan. I would train hard during the indoor season primarily to prepare for outdoors. We were not going to focus much on racing during the indoor season but rather use that time to gain strength and stamina for the intense workload and "fine tuning" that would come during the outdoor season. The focus was to peak at the right time. We had setup a few indoor races just to get my feet wet. Everything went to plan that indoor season and by the time April rolled around, I was ready to intensify my training and establish the final plan.

The key to setting the final plan began with setting the destination point. We looked at the racing calendar to determine which track meet would be the one where I'd have my best shot? It was determined that May 23rd, in Southern California at the "UCLA OPEN" would be the date. It was marked on the calendar and in my personal journal as the destination point. (When determining and writing down your destination point, try to be as specific as you can about what you intend to do on that day.) Here is what I wrote:

"On May 23rd, 1992 I will run the 1500 meters in under 3:41.80 seconds and qualify for the Olympic trials!!!"

Up until that point we had scheduled a race every two weeks. Then my Coach decided to add "Just in case" races. In the final two weeks leading up to the trials there was scheduled the "Last Chance" meets for anyone still hoping to qualify and make the standard for the Olympic Trials. They were both held on "back to back" weekends at the same location:

Northeastern University in Boston. I thought, "It's better to be safe then sorry" but I didn't believe I would need those races.

The intense training began and everything was going to plan. In my first outdoor track race at The University of Illinois in early April, I finished 5th in a time of 3:48.19. Not the best result but certainly not the worst. The weather was pretty rough and the wind was gusting. I am a firm believer in finding the positive from each experience. When we choose the perspective of, "What went right" instead of "What went wrong" it focuses our mind on the things that will continue to move us forward. This gives us "HOPE" and "HOPE" is a very motivating, inspiring and empowering ingredient in our lives. (Always try to cultivate HOPE whenever and wherever you can) The positives from this race were many. I felt comfortable throughout. I had a pretty strong finishing kick where I passed 4 guys down the home stretch. The pace was even and I felt I had a lot left at the end. All in all I felt good about it and was on my way!

Two weeks later was the next race at the University of Tennessee. My training had been going well but I had been pushing myself and was feeling fatigued going in. The race itself was interesting because although we started out pretty slow, we finished fast! I ended up 3rd in a time of 3:46.10. I was glad to see my time improve from the first race but I felt a bit concerned at how tired I was feeling. My Coach reassured me that with the training being as intense as it was the fatigue I was feeling should be expected. We were working right thru these early races in order to peak in late May thru June.

After another two weeks of strong and effective training I was ready to have a good race. This time I was in Madison at the University of Wisconsin. I was excited and nervous about this race because some of my old competitors would be there. I was also thinking that if the race went well I could qualify today! The University Wisconsin has a track with tighter turns and long straightaways. This could bode well for a fast time. We had beautiful weather and I was feeling confident. In the end, it was a good race. I finished 3rd once again but my time improved to 3:44.56. I was a little disappointed that I didn't go with the leader with a lap to go because he ended up qualifying running 3:41.50. I don't know why I didn't go with him when he broke from the pack. I felt pretty good yet I hesitated. I knew now that I'd be ready to leave it all on the track in two weeks at UCLA.

During the next two weeks leading up to the Destination Point where I plan on Qualifying for the Olympic Trials in the 1500 meters, my Coach had me really focus on my speed. I have a very good kick but my most effective quality is my explosiveness at the start of the kick. Not many runners have the quickness I have to make my move and then sustain it down the stretch. My Coach had the feeling that this could be the difference at the end of the race that could get me under that qualifying standard. He also knew that when my "Kick" was on, then I was extremely confident so that final week before the UCLA meet we honed my speed! I was ready!

When we arrived on the UCLA campus it was a gorgeous Southern California day. Mid 70's, sun shining and very little wind. These were ideal conditions for a fast race. When I saw who I'd be competing against my heart began to race and the butterflies emerged within the depth of my stomach because some of America's best milers were there. Everything was setup for me to qualify. This day and this race was the destination point in my plan. Now it was time to MAKE IT HAPPEN!

As I stood on the line in the 7th position I realized there were 13 other runners. This would be a crowded field so I had to get out safely and somewhere in the middle of the pack. We did have a "rabbit" in the race because many of the athlete's there believed this would be the race to qualify for the trials. The rabbit was set to take us out in 57 seconds for the first ¼ mile and 1:55 for the ½. It was a little faster then I wanted to go but if I sat somewhere in the middle of the pack I should come thru the ½ at about 1:56 or 1:57. Regardless, it was going to be a fast and steady pace. The starter took his position and the race was about to begin!

It's amazing what happens moments before the gun goes off. A calming stillness comes over you. The nerves and butterflies disappear and I think its because you are at the point of no return. It is now time to do what you've worked so hard for. It is your moment of truth. That is why when it comes to distance running, the most talented athlete is not always the winner. The runner who has put in the work, the miles, the intervals, they can be victorious because they have prepared. When you have, a certain confidence can come with it. It is a "knowing" that you are ready. I believe its also your bodies way of being still for one last moment because the burst of energy and adrenaline that's about to come is astounding! I was ready!!!

"Runners set...BANG"

We were off! There was a bit of jostling at the start but nothing too bad. In this race we were working together. Every competitor had one goal in mind...to qualify! I settled in the middle of the pack right around 7th or 8th position, right where I wanted to be. The first 2oo meters your trying to calm down from the adrenaline coursing thru your system. Once that happened, I began to relax and fixate on running comfortably and smoothly. As we passed the ¼ mile mark I heard the timer yell "55-56-57." We went out pretty fast and right we were supposed to be. The next 200 meters I moved up into 5th position and settled in along the rail. I was still feeling strong and very much in control. The first ½ of most mile/1500's are pretty simple. Stay calm and relaxed and try to keep the pace as even as possible. The key is to conserve as much energy for the 2nd ½ of the race. As we came down the home stretch approaching the 800 meter mark, I noticed one of the studs in the race, Jeff Atkinson who won the Olympic trials 1500 meters 4 years earlier was beginning to make a move to the lead. I quickly bolted around the guy in 4th place and got in right behind the top three who were closely following the rabbit. I knew once the rabbit dropped out that someone would make a move and it looked to be Atkinson. I had to be in position to go with this group. At 800 meters I heard the timer yell out, "1:54, 1:55, 1:56." We were right on pace as the 2nd half of the race began.

As we made our way down the backstretch I had to be careful because I was running directly behind the runner from Reebok, Steve Ave. Steve was not your typical middle distance runner. He was about 6 foot 3 with a stride that seemingly doubled mine. His back kick was coming dangerously close to my face! I decided I needed to go around him and into 3rd. That was easier said then done. As I made my move he did as well because he was going for the lead. That pushed me out into lane 3 for a few strides and it cost me some valuable energy. I let him surge to the lead and tucked back on the rail still in 4th position.

I felt I was in good position and I had to do was go with these three runners until the end. We had opened up a 10-yard gap on the rest of the runners. I was where I needed to be as we approached the ¾-mile mark. I needed to hear at least 2:57, 2:58. As we passed the timer yelled out, "2:55, 2:56!" Now comes the hard part, hanging on and kicking in strong to the finish. The Ave and Atkinson continued to duel for the lead position as we bolted down the back straight and another tall and gifted athlete, Charles Marsala was right in front of me. I looked tiny compared to these three. The advantage I had behind these guys was drafting off of them and getting dragged along to a fast time. As we entered the final 200 meters I pulled up alongside Marsala and focused on the back of Atkinson who was a couple of strides ahead of me and on the shoulder of Ave. If I could just keep in close contact with Atkinson I felt I'd hit the time I needed to qualify on the day I said I would. Off the final turn and into the home stretch I was now right on Atkinson's shoulder. Marsala had fallen back a few strides. Every muscle in my body ached as I struggled trying to fight thru the pain and not tie up. Ave had pulled away about 5 yards and I remained right on Atkinson's shoulder. I could now see the clock on the side of the track at the finish and I knew I just had to get under 3:41.80! The last 50 meters were a blur and as my body began to tighten all I could do was push thru it with everything I had. When we hit the finish line, Ave had won and Jeff Atkinson was a step ahead of me as I finished third. When I crossed the line I glanced at the clock and I saw 3:41 as I passed! I felt that I had it and as I went to my knees gasping for air I glanced up art the scoreboard and it read:

1. Steve Ave 3:39.78

2. Jeff Atkinson 3:41.25

3. Eddie Slowikowski 3:41.97

I couldn't believe it, I missed qualifying by 17 hundredths of a second!!!

THE IMPORTANCE OF CONTINGENCY PLANNING

After my race at UCLA I had to quickly regroup and create a new destination point. Some people refer to this as "PLAN B" or a contingency plan. If you recall, when My Coach and I sat down to create my action plan as well as the Destination Point, we factored in a contingency in case things didn't work out the way we planned. We had set two final races the last week in May and the first week in June just before the Trials in case they were needed. This type of thinking is very important when it comes to setting a plan for your goals because it allows for flexibility and the unexpected. I ran a personal best at UCLA breaking 3:42 for the first time and although I didn't hit my goal on that day, I felt more confident then ever that I could for how close I came. Setting a contingency plan is a "must do" in any planning or strategy session when it comes to your goals and getting results. Some might argue that a contingency plan could be put into step 5 of The Four Minute Formula, "Prepare for the Pain." I decided to put it in this step because ultimately we are looking to achieve our goals and reach those destinations and it is important to know that it might not work exactly to plan. A contingency plan can also relieve some of the pressure we may feel along the way. Just knowing that we have "backups" in place can go a long way to helping us perform at the highest levels when needed.

In the business world a contingency plan is put in place in the event of a disaster that disrupts a company's production and puts employees in danger. The idea behind such a plan is to safeguard data, minimize disruption and keep everyone as safe as possible. Although missing the qualification standard by .017 seconds doesn't qualify as a disaster, it certainly hurt. I was so grateful that my Coach had the wisdom and the foresight to put in place my contingency plan. Now it was onto Boston.

"LAST CHANCE TRACK MEETS"

I arrived in Boston on Thursday with the first of two final "Last Chance" races on the schedule. The Track meet was being held at Northeastern University. These races attracted all those runners who were still looking for a qualifying time and a few that wanted to sharpen their racing. We were less than 3 weeks away from the Olympic Trials and these were the final opportunities that could produce fast times. I headed out by myself this time because my Coach was at a collegiate meet with some of his athlete's at Loyola. It was a strange feeling being out there alone yet it seemed fitting. I was going to have to get this done by myself. I completely rested on Friday and took in the sites of Boston. On Saturday I woke up early and began my rituals of race day. Every athlete has their rituals they go thru on the day of the event. These rituals and habits help prepare you for optimal performance. They also help keep you "sane" as the nerves and pressure mount.

I made my way to the track about an hour before my race. That is typically when I'd begin my warm up rituals. The track stadium was about ½ full yet tons of people seemed to be milling about the infield area. Approximately 15 minutes prior to the race I heard the 1st call for the 1500meters. That's the cue to get my spikes on a do some striders. This is also the time when the nerves and pressure you feel seem to hit its plateau. With about 5 minutes to go I heard the 2nd call for my race. Then just a few minutes later they called all athletes to the starting line. We had 16 runners in my race and I recognized just a few. I was put in the 12th spot on the starting line and I knew it was again going to be crowded and intense at the start. Now comes the calm before the storm. I began to breathe deeply and try to relax. We were set… "BANG"

As we lunged off the line, the elbows were flying and there was a lot of jostling for position. I got knocked back a bit and I didn't feel like wasting too much energy fighting for my spot so I slowed down a step and headed toward the back and settled in around 14th position. This was not where I wanted to be but on the indoor circuit I always went to the back so it was something I was familiar and quite comfortable with. Being in the back meant that I'd have to be hyper aware of what was happening ahead of me. When I saw any kind of a gap begin to form I'd have to jump on it and improve my position. Just like the week earlier at UCLA, we had a rabbit pacing us for the first ½. I was a little worried that being so far back in the pack that I might not be where I needed to be after the ¼ mile. As we approached the completion of the first lap I heard the timer yelling the splits: "54-55-56!" We were out fast and being near the back had put me on pace with where I wanted to be. I decided once we made our way around the 2nd turn and down the back-stretch that I would begin to move up. I shot out into lane two off the 2nd turn and made my way into the 9th position. A small gap had formed right there so I quickly snagged that spot back in line and on the rail. The pace was still healthy but I felt comfortable. At the ½ the timer was yelling: "1:53-1:54-1:55!" We had maintained a strong pace and the rabbit did a superb job getting us out well. Just like the last lap I would wait until coming off the 2nd turn again to continue to move up. This time, I didn't have that luxury as a gap was forming between the top 5 runners and the rest of us. I made my move right then and there as I quickly moved around the few runners in from of me until I was on the tail end of the lead pack. Again I settled in on the rail. It's always at this point of the race where it feels like your running faster but in all actuality your slowing a bit. I just stayed where I was drafting off this lead pack. I knew for me to qualify I'd probably have to finish in the top three. I was in a perfect spot and I still felt pretty strong.

The pace quickened as we approached the ¾ mile. The timer was yelling out the splits: "2:55-2:56!" Right where we needed to be. Everyone stayed intact down the back- stretch and then with 200meters to go, one of the favorites in the race and a guy I was very familiar with, Mark Dailey burst to the lead! I was waiting for someone to make a move and there it was! I quickly responded and bolted by the guys in front of me and off the final turn we went. Dailey had a few yards on me as I pushed with al I had spring toward the finish. I got within a stride of Dailey and as we crossed the line 1st & 2nd place I saw the trackside clock and it read 3:41 as we passed. Once again it was going to be close. I just stood on the track anxiously awaiting the results on the scoreboard. After what felt like an eternity, suddenly they appeared.

1. Mark Dailey 3:41.54

2. Eddie Slowikowski 3:41.86

I missed by 0.06 seconds!

When I saw the result, it felt like all the air left my body. I made my way over to the grass on the infield of the track and simply sat down in disbelief. I was devastated. It felt like the running Gods were playing a bad joke on me. I was close to tears when out of nowhere the Coach at Georgetown, Frank Gagliano aka "Gags" who is a legend in the coaching world came up to me and said,

"Eddie, you ran a fantastic race! You looked great out there! Great Kick!!!" I looked up at him with the sadness and disappointment washing over me and said,

"I missed qualifying by 6 hundredths of a second." He quickly shot back with incredible exuberance, "I know I couldn't believe it!!! That is so close but your coming back next week right?" I replied, "I don't know I guess." Again with great excitement he said, "What do you mean you guess? You have to come back and you'll make it next week!!! I'll see you then!" He smiled a very reassuring smile, pat me on the top of my head and moved on. I just watched as he went up to athlete after athlete sharing encouraging words and his positive energy. Then I noticed something, everyone he left in his wake was smiling. He positive vibe was infectious and I began to think about what he said to me. I had one more chance. Why am I sitting here like my world has ended? I just ran another Personal Best! So I got up, grabbed my things and was now excited to come back in one week and GET THIS DONE!!! I now had a new destination point. I will qualify for the Olympic trials on Saturday June 12th!!!

As I began to make my way out of the track stadium, I was stopped by someone calling my name. I turned around and saw a guy I did not know coming toward me. He was decked out from head to toe in Reebok apparel. His name was Dave and he handed me his card. What he said next was totally unexpected.

"Great race today Eddie. I wanted to ask if you are planning on racing again next week? If so, Reebok would like to sponsor you as one of our athlete's...interested?"

I couldn't believe it. They wanted to sponsor me because they felt I'd make it to the Olympic Trials the following week. They were going to work out a deal with me as well as give me official gear to represent Reebok! They were also willing to keep me out there in Boston and pay for my entire week so that I could concentrate on getting ready for the race and not have to worry about travelling back and forth to Chicago. They were headquartered in Boston and felt it would give me my best chance at qualifying. This was AMAZING! I was now an officially sponsored athlete! More importantly, their faith in me was quite a confidence boost! I was no longer sad for missing the qualifying standard by 0.06, I was exhilarated to have one more opportunity and I planned to MAKE IT COUNT!

THE LAST CHANCE

That week flew by as I prepared for my final shot at qualifying. One great perk to staying out there that week was I was able to have a few workouts on the track where I'd be racing again at Northeastern. It helped me feel more comfortable and "at home" at this place. When the day finally arrived I felt good. I was well rested and I felt sharp. The Reebok guys took great care of me and it was just incredible how much support they gave all week. They picked me up in an official Reebok Van and we made our way to the track. I quickly learned that the 1500 meters would have 18 participants! That's a lot of runners in one race but I understood that people from all over the country were migrating to Boston for one last shot at qualifying. It was going to be crowded out there but I had become used to it. This however, would be the biggest field of runners I had ever raced in. I had been talking to my Coach all week about race strategy. The start would be key. A week earlier I got bumped off the start and literally pushed back and thus, had to settle in the back of the pack. That alone probably cost me the qualifying mark. We both knew that I had to get out off the line faster to make sure I was in better position that first lap. I certainly was quick enough so I just needed to be ready to bolt when that gun went off. The idea was to settle in about 10th position and to try to be on the rail if possible. Once I had established a good position the rest would be awareness of what was happening ahead of me and to keep contact with the leaders until the end. I had done a good job the previous week with that so I felt comfortable and confident with this game plan.

As we began to lineup I was thrilled that I was called in the 4th position on the starting line. This would give me a great opportunity to get out quick and get into position along the rail. I tell ya, I can't even explain what I was feeling at that moment on that starting line. There is something different knowing that THIS WAS IT. No more chances after this. I either get this done or I am done. I had feelings of all kinds running thru me but most of all I WAS SCARED. There come these moments in everyone's journey where you have no choice but to face your fear…This, was that moment for me.

"RUNNERS SET…BANG!!!!!!!"

I shot off that line quick and for the first 10 yards I was in the lead. I slowed to allow the rabbit to take over and he did. I slid back into 5th position on the rail and decided I was good and that this was a good spot for me. I was so full of adrenaline and I needed to calm down. I just focused on my breathing and my stride and after a few more seconds I began to feel in control. I was happy to stay right where I was and let the rabbit do his job. If we could keep it even like we had a week before I was confident I could qualify.

The first quarter was right where we needed to be at 56 seconds. There was no jostling and no drama thus far because everyone in essence was working together. We were pretty much in a single file line following the rabbit. The ½ mile point again was perfect as the timer yelled out, "1:54-1:55…" As the rabbit stepped off the track there was a slight hesitation as to who was going to take over the pace. Then from behind a runner named Daniel Maas bolted to the lead and took over. I believe he was from out East and he is a very respected runner. I moved up into 4th position and just held on. I began to feel a bit of fatigue in my legs but all I tried to focus on was the guys in front of me. At the ¾ mile mark I wanted to be at 2:55. The 4 of us out front had put a five yard gap on the next runners and as we passed, the timer yelled, "2:55-2:56!!!" I was right where I needed to be.

When I heard that split, I felt another wave of adrenaline and a burst of energy. It was going to come down to the kick. The 4 of us made our way around the third turn and as we approached the final turn I made my way onto the right shoulder of Greg Whitely who was moving up as well. As we shot off of that turn I was now in third and gaining on the leaders. With about 100 meters to go the clock on the side of the track was coming into view but at that moment I decided not to look. I told myself, "Forget the clock...win this race!" The rest was a blur as I reached down to the depths of my soul and simply gave it every thing I had. I hadn't even realized I was winning as I sprinted to the finish. I gave one last push, fighting to keep from my muscles tying up as I lunged toward the tape! When I crossed the line I immediately fell to my knees gasping for air, afraid to look up at the scoreboard. A few seconds later I mustered up the courage and looked.

1. Eddie Slowikowski 3:41.10

I DID IT!!! I QUALIFYED FOR THE OLYMPIC TRIALS!!!

The feeling I had when I realized I'd made it on the final day was one of exultation and relief. Most of all I was proud of myself. I had set out to do something and although it was an arduous journey that didn't always go to plan, I did it! These are the moments and achievements that no one can take away from you. They are the sweetest moments because I honestly earned it. I had worked, dedicated and persevered. Having a destination point allowed for me to understand what needed to be done and when. Having a contingency plan gave my endeavor flexibility and more possibility. I know it sounds cliché but all we can do is OUR BEST. I think we know when that's happening and I know we know when its not. Having your destination point will give your journey more clarity and purpose. That purpose will inform you that this day, the present moment is what you have and if you take action it may lead you toward something incredibly special and worthwhile. Make your plans and decide the date of your destiny. Then simply do all you can to realize it! (Oh and don't forget to leave room for a PLAN B)

*I wanted to share a quick side note about what happened at the trials. My race was the very next week after I had qualified. I had hit the "A" standard in qualifying which meant that United States Track and Field

Federation paid for my entire time for the duration of the trials. When the day of my Heat came, it was an incredibly hot and humid New Orleans day. I believe it was 90 degrees with 100% humidity. It was brutal. The race started out ok but I knew I was simply tired and emotionally drained. I had been thru a lot just to get there. At the half way-point of the race I was barely hanging on and with a lap to go I had nothing left to give. I did not advance past the first round. I did remain as a sponsored Athlete with Reebok and after the trials I became a "Reebok Ambassador" representing the company at many road races. Some years later, something occurred to me. My Dream was to make the Olympic Team but my Goal and my plan was to make theOlympic Trials. There's a big difference between the two.

STEP #7:

GIVE BACK TO THE WORLD

Mother Teresa was asked why she did the work she did in the slums of Calcutta and she said, "Because Everyday I see Jesus Christ in all his distressing disguises." Once you understand that she saw her "Savior" in all the people suffering around her, it's no wonder she dedicated her life to do WHAT SHE COULD to alleviate some of that suffering. We each can do our part to make a difference in our own unique way. Where do you feel a call to serve? What difference do you believe you could make? When you quiet your mind and listen to your heart you may hear another's cry for help. When you do, answer the call for there is a reason YOU are hearing it.

DO SOMETHING

It was the start of the 2nd semester of my freshman year at Loyola University Chicago and I was contemplating whether or not I should go to my Criminal Justice class. The reason for the hesitation was the weather. It was Chicago in early January and Loyola's north campus in Rogers Park sits right off of Lake Michigan. If you've never experienced winter in Chicago, especially a night with the wind whipping off the lake, then you don't know what this kind of cold is like. The temperature was 2 degrees with a wind chill of

-10. My class was at the downtown campus right in the heart of the city just off the magnificent mile and Michigan Avenue near the famed Water Tower Place. I had to take public transportation, which would mean I'd have to stand out at the bus stop and wait for the #127 to take me downtown. I really wasn't up for it but I also knew it was never good policy to miss class, especially the first one. So I decided to brave the elements and do what needed to be done.

As I stepped out into the cold I immediately felt it down to the bone. As I stood out at the bus stop I quickly began to regret my decision as my teeth clattered and my body shivered. I was the only one out there, looking foolish as I waited for the bus to emerge from around the bend. Finally, after what felt like an eternity (which was probably more like 5 minutes) the bus grumbled up to a hissing stop and I immediately jumped on board. Luckily on this night the heat was working and I began to thaw out. The bus lurched forward and began its journey downtown. The ride would take approximately 15 minutes. As it rolled along I began to think about the fastest and most efficient way to get off that bus and into Lewis towers where my class would be. I had it all figured out.

The bus finally pulled up right in front of Water Tower place on Michigan Avenue and when the doors opened the wind hit me like a slap in the face. I jumped off the bus, crossed Michigan Avenue, took a left turn to Pearson and then went right. The cold was so intense I could feel my muscles on the brink of cramping as I fought thru it to get indoors. I had about 100 yards to the entrance of Lewis Towers where my class and warmth was waiting. With about 50 yards to go something caught my periphery, it was a homeless man huddled in a stairwell across the street. He called out to me, "Hey Mister" I stopped dead in my tracks and looked his way. He motioned for me to come over to him. For a split second I contemplated what to do. Then within an instant the decision was made. I ignored him and ran into the building.

I arrived at my classroom a few minutes late and the professor had already begun lecturing as I quietly found a seat in the back of the room. While he was explaining the syllabus I found myself very distracted by my thoughts of the homeless man outside. I began to feel an anger rising up in me as I thought about him huddled in that stairwell in these elements. An irate voice in my head was screaming,

"What kind of world is it where a homeless person is outside trying to find shelter in a stairwell in sub zero temperatures freezing to death like an animal????!!!!"

I was really getting upset as the voice continued:

"This is insane! He is out there right now and nobody does anything! Nobody does anything!"

Then I'll never forget what happened next. A softer voice from deep within said,

"How come you didn't do anything?"

Without warning I couldn't breathe. My conscious was confronting me with the truth. I didn't do a thing. One thing I have discovered in life is that it is easy to point your finger at the world and blame it for the problems we see & experience. The harder thing is to take action and do something about it. I was raised in a home where service was not just talked about but was practiced over and over again and as I sat in that classroom I began to feel guilt and shame building within me. It didn't take long before I decided to do something.

I headed back out onto the street and approached the homeless man from behind. I'll admit that I was a little scared not knowing exactly what I was getting myself into. I couldn't focus much on my fear because of the bone chilling cold. I stopped about 10 feet from him and called out,

"Excuse me sir?"

I startled him as he turned quickly from his hunched over position in the stairwell. It took him a moment to gather himself and focus but when he did he smiled and said,

"Hey, you came back!"

In that moment the fear lifted for he was just an old man and nothing to be afraid of, so I stepped closer and said, "

Do you need some help? Is their anything I can do for you?"

He smiled and quickly asked,

"Do you got any money?"

I opened my wallet and all I had was one dollar...that was it. Disappointed I replied,

"No not really."

He then told me that he hadn't eaten in 2 days. When I opened my wallet I noticed a card I had in there from Loyola University that I used to receive my meals from in the cafeteria. I was on what's called a "Full Ride" College scholarship as an athlete at Loyola. What this meant was my entire College tuition was paid for as well as my room and board. When I'd eat I just had to present my card to the cashier and it would be taken care of. I did not have a chance to eat dinner that night therefore, a dinner was available. I showed him the card and told him this could get him something to eat right over in the cafeteria across the street. He smiled as I helped him to his feet and we made our way over to get some food.

When we walked into the cafeteria it was a Tuesday night so there weren't many people in there. A few people were drinking coffee and catching up on work. The looks I got made me feel uneasy because it was obvious I was bringing a homeless person into the cafe and the few that were there didn't like it. I tried my best to ignore them and we found an isolated table away from everyone. I asked him what he liked and was able to get him a full tray of food. I brought it over, placed it in front of him and sat directly across from him. He looked at me, smiled and looked at the food and began eating. He didn't look up for 10 minutes until everything on that tray was gone. When he finished he looked in my eyes and said,

"Thank You."

I looked at him and said,

"You're Welcome and if you don't mind me asking, why are you in that stairwell outside especially on a night like tonight?"

He leaned forward and his tired eyes looked at mine as he began to tell me his story:

"I've been homeless for almost 2 years now. Two years ago my life changed drastically. My wife of 43 years died of breast cancer. She battled that awful disease valiantly for a few years until it finally took her from me. She was the love of my life. She was all I had. We couldn't have children and I have no living relatives or family...its just me now. I had a good job as a mechanic for most of my life. I had retired 5 years ago. We did ok. We got by but when she got sick everything changed. The treatments she needed, the medications it was all so expensive. Our insurance covered some of the costs for awhile but after a year of her struggle they terminated the coverage, so we had to do whatever we could to continue the treatments, the chemo therapy, the medications needed to battle that disease. In the end, I went bankrupt and lost everything. After she passed, I was alone and had nothing left."

As he told me his story, I just couldn't believe this could happen to someone in The United States of America, the wealthiest Nation in the world. I was 18 at the time and pretty naive. I didn't realize that at that point in our history some 40 million people lived without health insurance because they simply couldn't afford it. In his case he had paid for health insurance his entire adult life and when it became expensive for the insurance company to pay the hefty costs, they just decided not to. This practice among insurers became fairly common and it destroyed people's lives. (That is why I firmly believe to this day that health care should be a right and not a privilege.) When he finished, I was speechless. I couldn't just leave it at that. I couldn't just send him back out to his stairwell and hope he didn't freeze to death. Now I was involved. We had to find a place for him to stay. He needed shelter. I went over to the yellow pages (which was our Google back in the day) and I looked up Homeless Shelters. It turns out there was one just a few blocks from where were. I called them up and asked if I could bring him over there. They said the Shelter was full but because of the unbearable conditions outside they had opened up the basement as an emergency shelter for people to get out of the cold. They said it was crowded but that we could squeeze him in. I told them that we would be there in 10 minutes.

As we made our way over to the Shelter in the brutal cold I had realized that we hadn't even officially met. I said, "My name is Eddie by the way." He reached out with his tattered gloved hand and replied, "I'm John." It didn't take long to walk the few blocks to get to the Shelter but we were both freezing when we arrived. It was a Catholic Church. We headed down the back stairs to the basement where we were welcomed in. When I stepped foot in that basement I was startled by what I saw. It was just an old, cold and poorly lit dingy basement with a cement floor and not much else. What startled me was not only how many people were down there (it was packed) but how many children I saw. In that moment I realized what a sheltered life I had lived because it just didn't dawn on me that I'd see children. There were little kids with their mothers. There were teens strewn about that I later learned were runaways and throwaways. (A throwaway is a teenager who was kicked out of their home) There were some crying infants and there were many individual adults of all ages and ethnicities. All they had were little blue mats with about an inch of padding (the kind they had in Gym class back in the day) some ratty old pillows and very thin and old blankets. I spoke to the man running the Shelter and I asked if there was anyway to get John a permanent place to stay. He deftly brought out a clipboard with a pen tied to it and explained how they had a waiting list and that people were coming and going all the time. He told us that he needs to sign this list and when his name comes up and there's an opening we will contact him and let him know a spot is available. He will have until 5pm that day to arrive and if he does he can stay in the permanent Shelter for awhile. Once in the system, they said that they'd work with him on getting some housing. The obvious question was, how would they contact him? He has no phone because he has no home. I decided to put my name on this list next to Johns with my phone number and I asked if they would call me when a spot comes available and I will make sure he gets here. They agreed. I handed the clipboard back, grabbed a blue mat, a pillow and a tattered blanket and helped John find a small piece of floor space to call his own. I told him to try and get some sleep and that I will come see him again soon. As I made my way to the exit I stopped to take one last look around. I caught the eye of a little African American girl who was leaning against her sleeping Mom across the room. She smiled and waved goodbye. I felt the rush of emotion come over me and I fought back the tears as I mustered up a meek smile and waved back. I left the basement of that Church and headed back to my warm dorm room and barely slept that night.

The next day at track practice, I stood before the team in the locker room and asked the guys if anyone had classes at the downtown campus throughput the week? Out of the 18 guys in that locker room, 10 hands shot up.

"Great! Would you guys do me a favor when you go down there? If you look across the street from Lewis towers, there is a stairwell that goes down into a basement door in the Quigley North building. I met a homeless guy named John last night who was living in that stairwell. When you go down there could you do me a favor and check on him and see if he's ok? I brought him to an emergency shelter last night because of the cold. Since today is a little warmer I'm pretty sure they closed the emergency shelter and sent people back on the street. If they did, I'd bet that John went back to his stairwell. When you go down there and check on him, introduce yourself, tell him that I sent you and if you can could you bring him something to eat?"

When I asked the question I felt a tinge of apprehension but I was quickly relieved because without hesitation all of my teammates agreed that they would. When the next Tuesday rolled around, I went to class an hour early so that I could get John something to eat and see how he was doing. He told me that he'd met a bunch of my teammates over the last week and that they were all so kind to him. They brought him so much food that he couldn't eat it all. Subsequently John ended up introducing a few of my teammates to some other homeless people he knew so that they could benefit from their generosity. I was so impressed and proud of my teammates! A few more days passed and I got the phone call from the Shelter saying that a spot is available for John and that if he is here by 5pm then he will have a place to stay. I promised that we would get him there. My teammates and I made a workout out of it, ran the 10 miles from the North campus to downtown, scooped up John and brought him to the shelter.

Once we arrived at the Shelter we got John all checked in and as he settled I began talking to the gentleman who was running the Shelter. He told me that the Shelter held about 40 residents. Once they have a bed they are allowed to stay as long as they adhere to the rules and while they are there, they have programs to help them get back on their feet and into some permanent housing. As long as they are checked in each day by 5pm they can keep their spot. He explained how people were coming and going all the time. Some have been there for quite awhile while others may last a day or two. I asked if there was any other way we could help out. He told me that you could donate and serve meals. He also said that they needed volunteers at times to stay overnight and help with the needs of the residents. I told him that I'd be willing to volunteer for a night. He told me that they needed someone the following night.

When the next night rolled around I found myself back at the shelter ready to serve. I had no idea what to expect and I was a bit nervous but once I got to meet and know some of the other volunteers and residents I began to feel more comfortable. My first task was to help serve dinner.

Someone had donated a catered meal from a place called Lee n Eddie's. I remember the name because my name was part of the catering company. It was a great meal! It consisted of fried chicken, mashed potatoes and gravy, coleslaw, potato salad and brownies & jell-o for dessert. It was really good! When I asked the woman who donated it I was surprised to hear it was only around $150. This was more than enough food for everyone. In fact, many came back for a second helping. When the meal was done I cleared the tables and began washing dishes. Once that was completed a bunch of the volunteers left and it was now down to just me and one other person to stay and take care of whatever the residents may need throughout the night. This became the most rewarding part of the experience for me because before many of the residents decided to "turn in" I had the chance to get to know them. Like John, the people I met had stories that would just break your heart. It was from that experience that first night I volunteered that I began to appreciate and understand the phrase:

"There but for the Grace of God go I."

I came to realize just how lucky and blessed I had been in my life. Some people's circumstances were simply brutal and I wondered how I would hold up under similar situations? I just tried to listen with compassion and no judgments. I was intrigued to learn that some of the residents had jobs because one of my responsibilities was to make sure they were up in time to get to those jobs. My pre conceived notions of what a homeless person was or looked like were completely obliterated because that night I learned that it could truly be anyone of us. I realized that night how imperative it is not to judge but to listen. Not to condemn but to understand. Not to ignore but to serve. I'll be honest I didn't sleep that night. I just stayed up making sure that I take my responsibilities seriously while trying to be there for the residents. When my shift was done, I headed back to my dorm. I was invigorated yet exhausted and as I lay in my bed I thought of all the incredible people I had met in the last 24 hours and the experience I'd had. As I drifted off to sleep in the middle of the morning I did so with a grateful heart.

At track practice that afternoon I told my teammates of my experience at the shelter. They were very intrigued to hear all about it. I also thanked them for their compassion and generosity towards John. They were all so glad to hear that he was now settled in at the Shelter and being taken care of. I also told them about what I learned in terms of serving a meal. I explained to them how a really nice lady named Mary had donated the meal we served. It was from a caterer called "Lee n' Eddies" and that all it cost was around $150 bucks. I also explained how good it was and how it served every member of that shelter. The best thing however is that the catering company actually delivers the food so all you have to do is pay the bill and they'll bring it to wherever you need it. I asked the guys if they'd be willing to go in with me, pay for the meal and serve it at the shelter? Once again without hesitation my teammates unanimously said "LET'S DO IT!" So we picked a night for the following week, called the Shelter to let them know and then called Lee n' Eddies. A few days later my teammates and I were serving that same great meal to the residents of that Shelter. Talk about a great teambuilding and bonding experience. I was so proud of my teammates! (This is why when I work with organizations on Team Building I have them choose a charity in which they can serve together because I know how those experiences will bring them together.)

A few years later during my senior year was when I broke the Four Minute Mile. My time of 3:58.62 ranked as the #1 indoor mile time in the Nation indoors that year. This was a pretty big deal because the Chicago Tribune, a major newspaper in the city of Chicago, wanted to do an article about me! A reporter who was well known in Chicago for being on a TV show called "The Sports Reporters on TV" named Bill Jauss did the interview. During the interview I told him about the volunteer work my teammates and I had been doing at the homeless shelter. I told him about the night I met John. He was very intrigued by this and he decided to make this story and our volunteer work the main focus of the article. In fact, the next time we were scheduled to serve a meal he sent a photographer to take some pictures. When the article came out it was entitled,

"LOYOLA'S NEW STAR MILER IS A HUMANITARIAN, TOO"

In the article, Bill Jauss wrote of my journey from that first night my freshman year meeting my homeless friend to getting my teammates involved and the times we served together. The article had a "side by side" photo of me running and me serving food at the shelter. It spoke of my accomplishments on the track but it truly captured the service minded mentality we had adopted as a team. I was so proud of that article, not because of the running accomplishments but because of the heartfelt way he captured how my teammates and I were trying to make a positive difference in our world. That article had a huge response as the reporter who wrote it informed me how people were calling the paper asking where they could donate? The Shelter itself received many calls from people wanting to donate and volunteer after reading the article. The best part of it all however, is what became of John. The true heroes were the people working in those shelters day in and day out dedicating their lives to helping people get back on their feet. John stayed in the shelter system for quite awhile. Eventually they were able to get him into a halfway house and then his own apartment. They were able to get him government assistance and a part time job. John had his life back!

Every now and then I think of him. I remember that fateful frigid January night. I think back to the moment we saw each other and he motioned for me for help and how initially I ignored him. I remember the moment in that class when the angry voice inside me is yelling at the world asking the question "Why doesn't anybody do anything?"

I think back to that softer voice asking the question "Why didn't you do anything?" Then I remember the moment I realized I needed to DO SOMETHING. I often wonder what would have happened if I just listened to that first irate voice within and sat apathetically doing nothing? How would my life be different? The moment I decided to take action was the moment an incredible ripple of change began to take place. My friend

John's life was affected by those ripples as were my teammates but one life that was profoundly affected was mine. From this experience, I began to understand the power of service like I never had before. My relationships and friendships with my teammates had deepened and been enriched by serving together. I began to know a purpose in my life that would sustain me and bring out my "Better Angels" throughout my journey. This gave my life such abundance, joy and deeper meaning. It brought out the best in me. I wondered, "Where did that second voice, the one that inspired me to take action come from?" Is it in all of us? What do we need to be aware of to be able to hear it? How am I being called to "serve" in my life? The answers were within my story.

I was born into a strict Catholic family on the South Side of Chicago. My Father is 100% Polish and my Mother is 100% Irish. If you know anything about the Southside, you learn that you are not identified by your neighborhood but rather by your Catholic Parish. Catholicism is practically a prerequisite on the Southside. As far back as I can remember we never missed Sunday Mass. We never missed a Holy Day obligation and me and my siblings all had to go thru Catechism. (That's Sunday school to my Non-Catholic Brethren) And although today I am what you call a "lapsed Catholic" and have a lot of issues with the Catholic Church, my life in that religion is a big part of who I am. (You may leave the Church but the Church don't leave you) One thing I've always liked about the Catholic faith is its devotion to service. In Catholicism we believe the way you get closer to God is thru service to others. The Psalms inform us that we are "instruments" of Gods Love & Peace. It's our "good works" on Earth that will get us to the Kingdom of Heaven. I always liked that because it was one of the few things that made sense to me. It also meant that when it came to my Faith that I had something to say about it. How I live, how I serve the world would in essence my Faith. Both my parents believed very much in this and so they raised us accordingly. Once a month as a family we would pick a day do some sort of service. We would volunteer at soup kitchens, shelters, hospitals and nursing homes to name a few. One particular experience stays with me to this day. My Mom had decided that we would bake cupcakes and cookies and bring them to the Nursing home in town. When we arrived my Mom had me hold the cupcakes. We walked in and as my family headed into the hospitality room, I was left behind and cornered in the lobby by an elderly resident in a wheel chair. She rolled up to me as I backed against the wall. She had gotten a whiff of the chocolate cupcakes I was carrying and she wanted them! I was petrified and I couldn't move. She then proceeded to grab a cupcake and like a Python she opened her mouth and swallowed it whole! Then she grabbed another and another and another. I was paralyzed as she made that tray of cupcakes her very own. After her sixth or seventh, a nurse finally saw the "Cupcake Assault" and she ran over and yelled for me to STOP because SHE was DIABETIC!!!!" The nurse yelled this at me as if I was distributing her the cupcakes. And what the hell is diabetic??? I had nothing to do with it! Finally a large male orderly pulled her away and I was freed from the wall.

Now that was a funny yet traumatic experience from my younger years of service but what I remember most from our family service adventures was the feeling I'd have while serving. It felt good! I felt what it feels like to contribute something positive to another. I felt as though in a small way we were making a difference and that feeling has stayed with me and I'm sure it was because of my upbringing. That emphasis on service compelled me to go back out to John that fateful night. The University I attended was Catholic run by the Jesuits. Loyola University continued an emphasis on service throughout my time there. Each Sunday the student community would go to Mass at 10:30pm and some of the priests we had at Loyola were phenomenal speakers. Their Homilies could be incredibly inspiring. After one particularly inspiring night I went the next day to campus ministry and signed up for what was called an "Immersion Experience" in the city of Detroit. At the time in 1988, Detroit was a very rough city known as the murder capital of the United States. People in the inner city were really suffering and homelessness was at an all time high. A group of us from Loyola were heading in for a long weekend to serve in the Homeless Shelters there.

When we arrived we stayed in a convent right in the heart of the inner city. We'd get up in the morning and have breakfast and then head to a Shelter. Those drives through the streets of Detroit were very eye opening. Most of the homes were vacant and burnt out. The night before Halloween was known as "Devil's Night" in Detroit. It is like a night straight out of the movie "The Purge." Vandalism and Arson are the primary activities on that night and incredible damage is done ironically in the poorest of neighborhoods. We were there around Thanksgiving so the damage was new. The conditions that some in that city were living in were truly terrible. Once we arrived at the shelter we were charged with preparing and serving the food and cleaning the shelter. We'd serve from 8am until 7pm in the evening. Afterwards we would head back to the convent and talk about our experience. It was there that we'd share about the people we met and our experiences of the day. The most significant thing that struck me was the level of poverty that exists right here in America. I've seen it now in two major cities and realized how serious this problem was. I began to understand that there is a "GREAT DIVIDE" that exists in America between the "Haves" and the "Have Not's." I also realized that charity was not going to solve the problem. When you are born into poverty it is not just an economic issue because there is also a poverty of the Soul. When you are caught in the cycle of poverty it can be very hard to escape. Not everyone can just pull themselves up by their bootstraps. When you don't have anyone there to show you another way then how does one understand what to do to change it? Some of the people I'd met, after hearing their story helped me begin to realize how "unequal" things can be. The opportunities were just not there. I felt so very bad for many of them. I had deep sympathy but I certainly didn't have empathy for I have never had to experience anything like what the people I met in Detroit had to deal with on that immersion trip. As much as I tried to "immerse" myself in their situation it was painfully obvious that I was swimming in a different pool, a pool of privilege. It motivated me to want to do something more.

CYCLE

The definition of the word "Cycle" is a series of events that are regularly repeated in the same order. I mentioned the "cycle of poverty" before which is the belief that the set of factors or events by which poverty, once started, is likely to continue unless there is outside intervention. Seeing firsthand the situation some were dealing with helped me realize that serving in a way that could help create opportunities for people would be a better use of my time. My heart ached the most for the children born into poverty. It seemed that if intervention can happen in their lives then they'd have the best chance to break the cycle of poverty that they were born into. I always felt that education was the "Silver Bullet" to create those opportunities. After my trip to Detroit, I went to the Campus ministry and said that I'd like to try and help on a deeper level. My good friend Brenda, who ran the Campus ministry told me of a program coincidentally called "CYCLE!" This was a mentoring/tutoring program for kids in one of the most dangerous and drug addled projects in the city of Chicago called Cabrini Green. The "Cabrini Green Projects" were handled by the Chicago Housing Authority. It had a reputation as one of the most violent areas of the city. At its peak it housed over 15,000 people in mid and high-rise apartment buildings. The Projects were created to increase the availability of affordable housing for low-income families. The concept primarily failed because the projects radiate dysfunction and social problems that damaged local businesses and property values. They were also failing because of the lack of opportunity for those living there. The Drug trade would prosper and Gangs would find a way to controlling the area mostly thru intimidating and violent means. The Projects became a very dangerous place to exist. The "Cycle" program decided to set up shop right adjacent to the Projects because of the overwhelming need. Kids from Cabrini Green could join this program and receive services that will help them with education and opportunity. The commitment from the volunteer would be once a week for 2 hours in the evening. The way it worked was you'd be partnered with a child and every Tuesday night you would help mentor and tutor them in hopes of helping them with their education. The goal of the program was to keep the kids in school in hopes of not only graduating from High School but to help them get into College. If the child could get accepted to a college or University then the CYCLE PROGRAM would pay their tuition! When I heard that this was the commitment to the kids, I knew that I wanted to be involved. This was a chance to truly break the cycle of poverty while creating a new positive cycle of possibility! I was in.

A few weeks later I headed to the orientation for volunteers. I'll admit that I was concerned when I learned that the orientation and the place we'd be going every Tuesday night was the elementary school in the neighborhood just a couple blocks outside Cabrini Green and in a very violent and dangerous part of the city. I had no idea what to expect and I'll be honest, I was afraid. I wasn't going to let my fear stop me. Getting to the school wasn't that big a deal and although it was 6pm it was still light out and seemingly safe. Once in the school we all met up in the library. It felt like an awkward Junior High dance because they lined up the 23 volunteers on one side of the library and the 23 students on the other side. On this first night we were all going to be paired with our student. As they read off the names I watched as volunteer and student came together and met for the first time. 19 of the 23 volunteers were white while all 23 students were African American. You could see the apprehension on the faces of the students whom I'm sure had ample reason to doubt whether this person would be committed to this process. Many of them come from a world where the norm is people who are supposed to be there for you aren't. I'm sure one of the biggest hurdles would be gaining this child's trust. Eventually I heard my name:

"Eddie Slowikowski, your student will be Kenneth Crawford."

Kenneth was a 13 year-old boy who had known no life but the world of Cabrini Green. He had escaped the world of drugs & gangs thus far because of the strength of his Grandmother and now he was heading into his freshmen year of high school. Kenneth was a very quiet and unassuming boy. You could tell right from the get go that he was very guarded not knowing what to expect from this program. Admittedly, he had very little contact with white people and I could see that he had a "sadness" behind his eyes that suggested he had endured a tough life. The hardest thing would be gaining his trust.

That first night we just got to know each other. I did most of the talking and Kenneth just listened. He did share that he had 4 siblings. His older brother was in jail and he had two younger sisters. He lived with his Grandmother. He hadn't seen his Mother in the last 2 years and he had never known his Father. (I later discovered that his Mother was a drug addict and basically lived on the streets.) The program had a bunch of board games to play, something to help "break the ice." Kenneth and I sat down to play connect four. As we played game after game Kenneth would open up a bit more. I even was able to make him smile just before the end of the night. When the night was over, I shook his hand and said, "I'll see you next week!"

When next Tuesday rolled around I was back at CYCLE right on time and anxiously waiting for me in the library was Kenneth. When I walked in Kenneth immediately smiled and sprang to his feet to greet me. I could see the relief in his eye's as I'm sure he wondered if I'd come back. I knew in that moment that this concept was really about "showing up" more than anything else. That night, the program had a panel to discuss how to break free of the cycle of poverty to create a successful life. They had 8 adults on this panel all of which were once children living in the Cabrini Green Projects who had made it out and were now living lives as professionals in various fields. As each person on that panel spoke, it was very inspiring to hear what they had overcome. The point of the panel was to not only talk about their success but to talk about how they made it from where they were to where they are now. It turns out that a couple of the panelists were once part of the CYCLE program. They talked about what they believed were the most important factors that helped them make it out of Cabrini Green. The first common denominator that they all agreed upon was education. They encouraged the kids to work hard in school and focus on trying to get into college. The 2nd thing that they all shared in common was the one that has always stayed with me. They said that they each had one caring adult outside of their families that came into their lives and truly cared about them. Some spoke of the Boys and girls clubs of America, some spoke of programs at their Church and of course some spoke of the CYCLE program. They shared eloquently on how much that meant to them. Some of them shared how the Mentor they had was white and it had been the only personal contact they'd ever had with an adult from a different race. They talked about how the care and compassion that was shared with them was truly transformative. Each one on that panel said they believed that without that support and belief from someone outside of their families that they wouldn't have made it. That mentorship and more importantly that friendship told them they were more valuable then they'd ever realized. One of the panelists summed it up beautifully with this statement:

"Having this person in your life who cared and who showed up helped not only how I felt about myself but it helped me realize a future that I didn't know existed for me."

When I heard this, I knew that this required my commitment. Kenneth had already experienced enough abandonment in his life, and I knew that I couldn't be just another person who let him down. Kenneth and I worked together in the CYCLE program for 4 years meeting every Tuesday night. Along the way we developed a wonderful friendship and I came to really care about him. Those Tuesday nights were not just about tutoring, they were mainly about being part of each other's lives. He went through some pretty rough times during those years but he managed to make his way thru. Some of the things he shared with me about what his daily existence was like were truly frightening and each Tuesday I would be filled with anxiety as I waited to see him again. When he'd walk thru that door each week a wave of relief would pour over me. Some nights I'd be there just to listen as he dealt with some pretty horrific stuff and some nights we'd get a lot done toward his education. Sometimes the program would allow us to take our student out for a fun evening. Kenneth and I would always go bowling. Kenneth just loved to bowl! We had many wonderful experiences together and made memories I'm sure neither one of us will ever forget. Kenneth went onto graduate high school and instead of pursuing college he decided to pursue a life in law enforcement. The CYCLE program helped pay for the training and academy program and eventually Kenneth became a deputy Sheriff in Cook County. He was able to break the cycle of poverty in his family and he moved out of the Cabrini Green Projects. We kept in touch for a while after the program until eventually we lost touch. I look back on those years with great fondness and I wonder how my friend is doing. When I think about the experiences we shared, a smile comes to my face and a feeling of gratitude for the chance to be part of his life. I felt like I made a difference in his life but one thing I know for sure, he made a difference in mine!

THE MLK INFLUENCE

The date was January 21st, 1991 and I was sitting in the main chapel on the north shore campus of Loyola University Chicago where I had graduated from 6 months earlier. Madonna Della Strada is a beautiful basilica type structure right on the shores of Lake Michigan. I was there on this day to hear a priest named Michael Pfleger give a talk on **"A CALL TO SERVICE"** for today was Martin Luther King junior Day. Martin Luther King jr is one of my heroes. I have studied his life for many years and am very inspired by who he was in our world. In fact, in the questionnaire that I give people to understand the power of their personal role models, he is my answer to question 5:

"If you could sit down to dinner with any historical figure you've ever learned about in your life, who would it be?"

Inevitably when people ask, "Why him?" I tell them as a speaker I find him to be the most passionate, authentic & influential speaker I've ever heard. If I could sit with him I would love to talk with him about how he crafted his presentations. Where did he derive his idea's from? What inspired him to say the things he did? These were all questions that fascinate me but the main reason I would love to have dinner with him would be to ask him a single question regarding his final speech. That question would be this:

"How did you know your life was about to end?"

Before we can fully appreciate the meaning and power of his final speech, we need to examine what was happening in his life at that time. Dr. king was in Memphis because of a garbage strike. The African American sanitation workers in Memphis had gone on strike because of the unsafe work environment they found themselves in. He was also there as part of his **"Poor People's Campaign."** His friends had said that at that time Dr. King seemed to be a bit depressed which was unusual for him. He had been getting a lot of death threats and although this was nothing new, it seemed to be getting to him. He felt as though he was "coming down" with something and wasn't feeling well. His friends would say the only time Dr. King would not feel well was and lacked energy was when he was emotionally exhausted. While he was in Memphis he promised to come to Mason Temple on the evening of April 3rd to give a speech at a rally for the striking sanitation workers. When that night rolled around Dr. King was exhausted and not up for it so he asked his right hand man and best friend, Ralph Abernathy, a gifted orator as well to go give the speech. Ralph agreed and told Martin to get a good nights rest at the Motel.

When Ralph arrived at the church there was a terrible storm and masses of people were huddled outside trying to stay dry. Ralph wondered why they just didn't go into the Church. When Ralph entered Mason Temple he quickly realized why they hadn't gone in. They couldn't fit! The Temple was packed. Throngs of people had come out to hear Dr. King's message. When Ralph saw this he didn't have the heart to tell the organizers that Dr. King was not coming so Ralph got on the phone and called back to the Lorraine Motel. He said,

"Martin, you would not believe the crowd that has come out tonight to hear you speak! It is packed to the rafters! They didn't come to hear me. Are you sure you can't get down here and give the speech?"

Dr. King decided to leave the Motel and head down to the Temple. Once Dr. King arrived an hour and a half late, he was worried because he had nothing prepared. Ralph decided to help out and said that he'd go first and introduce Dr. King allowing him some time to figure out what he wanted to say. Ralph got up and introduced his friend with an impassioned speech that lasted close to an hour. Then it was Dr. King's turn. As he made his way to the podium and the throngs of microphones that lay before him he looked tired. He paused as the storm raged outside almost seeming as though he didn't know what to say. Then he began completely speaking off the cuff, which was something he was incredibly gifted at doing. He spoke for close to an hour building and building momentum and gaining energy as he went along. As his voice grew louder and more passionate the audience responded and something spectacular was unfolding. Then he came to the closing. These are the exact words he proclaimed in the final minute of the final speech he would ever give:

"Well, I don't know what will happen now. We've got some difficult days ahead. But it really doesn't matter with me now, because I've been to the mountaintop. And I don't mind.

Like anybody, I would like to live a long life. Longevity has its place. But I'm not concerned about that now. I just want to do God's will. And

178

He's allowed me to go up to the mountain. And I've looked over. And I've seen the Promised Land. I may not get there with you but I want you to know tonight, that we as a people will get to the Promised Land! And so I'm happy, tonight. I'm not worried about anything I'm not fearing any man. Mine eyes have seen the glory of the coming of the Lord."

As I write what he said I have tears in my eyes thinking about the sheer power and passion of those words. The chill and adrenaline of inspiration that I feel is undeniable as my heart lays heavy in my chest filled with sadness knowing that this is the end. This speech informs me that he knew what was coming and all he wanted to do was inspire others to continue on and never give up the quest for equality and respect through the power of Love and Compassion. Notice he did this by invoking hope and to quote one of my favorite movies, "The Shawshank Redemption"

"Hope is a good thing, maybe the best of things and no good thing ever dies."

Dr. King knew that hope and inspiration will live on long after he has gone and its this hope and inspiration that will be the fuel, the energy to keep moving forward. But how did he know his journey was ending? What was he in touch with within himself that kept him pursuing justice through LOVE when so much HATE was all around him? This is what I'd ask him. This is why I'd love to have met him. Today in my life as a speaker and consultant I try my best to emulate the example Dr. King set by learning all I can about who he was and what he believed in. This is what our heroes can do for us and how they can contribute to teaching us how to live our BEST LIFE!

Back at Madonna Della Strada the guest speaker, Father Michael Pfleger was stepping to the front of the altar to speak. He is a very well known priest especially in Chicago for his activist work for African Americans. He is a White Catholic priest and Pastor of a mostly African American Parish on the Southside of Chicago. He is also a lightning rod for controversy in the Catholic Community. Regardless of ones opinion of him, he is an amazing speaker. I had never heard him speak before and was very excited when I learned that he would be on the Loyola campus for this special day. I had other reasons for attending...I was depressed. Since I had graduated from Loyola University I was really struggling. My girlfriend broke up with me and I felt that my life was in limbo. I was supposed to be training as a professional runner preparing for the track season and although I was selected to be on one of the Nike teams, I hadn't been working out and running the way I needed to be. I was really feeling lost.

I entered the Chapel about 15 minutes prior to the beginning of the special mass and the place was already packed. Luckily, I found a single seat unoccupied in the fourth row center, so I snagged it. I sat and looked at the program waiting for things to begin. Once the program was sufficiently read and all the latest bulletins on campus were left in my memory I began to take in the beautiful surroundings of this Chapel where I had spent many hours the past 5 years. The beautiful stain glass windows, the stunning architecture. This place had been such a refuge for me. It had become a place where I really felt a sense of peace. Then the music began and they were ready to begin. Once we got thru the ritualistic portion of the Mass, the first & second reading and the gospel, it was now time for the homily. For those of you who are not Catholic, this is the Priests opportunity to deliver his sermon, which is usually based on the Gospel reading from that week. Father Pfleger did not stand behind the altar or the lectern. He came out in front of the Altar to be closer to his congregation. He began with the story of The Good Samaritan. This story is about a traveler who is stripped of clothing, beaten and left for dead along the side of the road. First a priest comes by but he simply avoids the Man. Then a Levite comes by but he to ignores the wounded Man. Finally, a Samaritan happens upon the suffering Jewish traveler. Historically it is important to know that the Samaritans and Jews despised each other, but the Samaritan stops and helps the injured man. A more modern telling of this is done in the following story.

"A guy is walking down the street and he slips and falls into a hole. The walls are so steep that he can't get out. A doctor walks by and the guy yells up, Hey Doc, I'm stuck down in this hole, can you help me out? The doctor writes out a prescription throws it down in the hole and moves on. Then a Priest walks by. The guy again yells up to the Priest, Hey Father I'm stuck down in this hole, can you help me out? The Priest writes out a prayer, throws it down in the hole and moves on. Then a friend comes by. The guy yells up, A Joe, I'm stuck down in this hole, can you help me out? So the friend jumps down in the hole. The guy looks at him in disgust and says, 'what the hell did you jump down in here for? Now we're both stuck down here." The friend replies, "Yeah but I've been down here before and I know the way out."

This little parable is about empathy. The deeper understanding of what someone else may be feeling or experiencing because you've been thru something similar. Father Pflegers Sermon about the Good Samaritan was focused around the power of Empathy and Action! He went on in his thunderous tone to remind us of the incredible life of Empathy, Action, Compassion and Love that Doctor King lived. He used his sermon as a call to action. He explained how Gandhi was a role model to MLK Jr. and it was thru the life and example of Gandhi that had in part inspired Dr. King to seek justice thru non-violence. It is amazing how we all have teachers and mentors who help show us the way. The example one can set could create ripples of change and influence that can echo for eternity. By the end of the sermon I was so inspired I knew I just had to do something. I left that Church and went directly to a homeless shelter about 20 minutes away and asked, **How can I help?"** They immediately put me to work cleaning up the kitchen before the dinner rush. Then they had me help prepare the food, sweep the floors and set the tables with paper plates and Styrofoam cups. We set out about 120 settings anxiously awaiting the opening of the door and the onslaught of very lonely and hungry people. When they finally closed the kitchen doors that night about 3 hours later, we had served 141 people. I met Men, Women, Teenagers and little kids. All of which having one thing in common, they each had no home to go to. The shelter had space for 80 people to stay and sleep. Therefore, we had to watch as 41 people had to head back out to the harsh Chicago winter. I went back to my apartment and I couldn't sleep. I realized I had been so very blessed in my life in ways I had simply taken for granted. I have never faced the type of adversity that the people I served that night had. I knew then that whatever I did in my life I would do what I could to bring goodness to this world while trying to relieve what suffering I could. This was not some new concept for me, this was something that was bred into the fabric of who I was. Service has played a major role throughout my life and it has given me some of the richest and deepest experiences I've ever had. Finding a way to serve the world is the key to experiencing our most fulfilling life.

As I stated before, one of our family service trips would be to nursing homes. My Father liked to go there and converse with the residents because of the incredible stories they told and the lessons therein. My Dad used to say, "When you're in the presence of a wise soul, you never forget it." On one particular trip we met an elderly gentlemen named Ed. I remember him because his stories were incredible and we shared the same name (although I've always gone by Eddie) My Dad and I sat with him for a long while as he told us stories of fighting in WWII and living thru the depression. He talked in great detail about a beach called Normandy and how he lost countless friends on that day. He talked about liberating people in France and although it was like a "living hell" the camaraderie & brotherhood he felt for his fellow soldiers were some of the greatest experience of his life. He was a very affable gentlemen and very kind. He was quite animated in his story telling and I just remember how interesting he was. I also remember the warm hug he gave me when we left and the look on his face as he said,

"Thank you so much for visiting with me."

Like many of the residents there, I believe he was pretty lonely. He didn't speak of his family and we didn't ask. I'm not sure to this day if he had family but I know he was sad to see us leave. On our way home I remember the talk my Dad had with all of us. He said,

"Kids I hope you understand a little more deeply how important it is in life to give of yourself to others."

He wasn't talking about money or charity he was talking about the sharing of oneself with another. Creating those meaningful connections is what truly saves people. That day was one of many profound experiences I had with service and with my family. I believe we made an authentic connection with those we'd met along the way. In the end, the richness and fullness of our lives come from the deep and meaningful connections we make with others.

I was very fortunate to go to College on a "Full Ride" athletic scholarship to Loyola University Chicago. That institution is run by the Jesuit order of the Catholic Church. The Jesuits are known for a deep emphasis on education and service. At Loyola we had plenty of opportunities to serve. I'm sure because of the experiences I'd had with my Family volunteering to serve, I had learned to get to know the people I was serving. During my Immersion trips back at Loyola, I would always take time to sit with some of the people and just talk with them as they ate. I would try to keep it light and learn a little about "who" they were. Many times they'd share and ask me about myself. It was those simple moments that I remember, breaking bread and just hanging out together. I'm sure for many that were there they just wanted to feel cared for. They just wanted to know that they mattered. Sometimes just recognizing another's humanity is all we need to do to help someone feel their worthiness. It's in those little moments spent with another who is suffering and taking the time to learn their story that we show respect. Listening to their journey helped me realize how blessed and lucky I have been throughout my life to have the love and support from so many as I made my way thru this world. When you come to realize that not everybody has that, it makes me wonder, who I would be without them? Service is not just about giving and compassion, it's also about perspective and receiving. For the perspective I have gained thru service, the things I've received from others thru service has been without question some of the most amazing gifts I've ever experienced.

I'll never forget on our final night of one of the many immersion trips I'd had, we all sat together and talked about our Faith. When people talk about their Faith, I always seek to discover why they believe what they do and how it compels them to live. My Faith has always been directly connected to service. To be that "instrument" of my higher powers Love & Compassion is what deepens my faith and my connection to the humanity around me. As our discussion continued, we were all asked to share something with the group that helps define what our faith means to us. Some people told a story, some shared a prayer. I decided to share a song. It was a song I had loved for a long time but I had never really thought of it in the context of my spirituality and Faith. When I listened to it again, I thought about God, higher power, whatever you personally call it and how it inspires me. How it inspires me to strive to be an instrument of love and compassion. Here is a line from the song that sums it up and how I feel about that spiritual presence in my life:

"If anyone should ever write my life story, for whatever reason there might be. You'll be there between each line of pain and glory cause you're the best thing that ever happened to me. You're the best thing that ever happened to me. You're the best thing that ever happened to me!"

Service can be a great way to deal with the blues. Whenever I get down or am feeling depressed, one thing that has always helped is volunteering somewhere. When I help someone less fortunate then myself, I receive the gift of perspective. This was never more "True" for me then when I was in my early twenties. I had qualified for the Olympic Trials in New Orleans but failed to make the team. My running career was in limbo and my girlfriend shortly thereafter broke up with me. I was heart broken on many levels and I felt lost. I really didn't know what I wanted to do outside of running, but I was going to have to decide soon. When you feel depressed there is literally no motivation to do anything. I was struggling. Then while walking around my old campus at Loyola University after a meeting with my Coach I decided to stop in at the University Ministry office. Back when I was a student at Loyola this is was a place I'd come to often because the people there were like family and they were always finding new ways to serve others. I went in there and sat on the old reliable comfortable couch that had been there for years and began talking with my friend Brenda. I told her that I wasn't doing so well and without hesitation she said,

"I've got the perfect thing for you Eddie!"

The following week I found myself in a Catholic Church on the South side of Chicago with a group of about 30 strangers. We were all waiting to see what this week was going to be about. The "perfect thing" my friend at the ministry center had in mind for me was a service retreat that would last a week. The idea was I'd spend my days working at a location that would be determined at the retreat and I'd spend my nights hanging out with my fellow attendees talking about spirituality, our experience and life. I figured I had nothing else going on and with the way I was feeling I could really use a change of scenery. The people around me were of various ages ranging in age from early 20's to mid 60's. It was a real diverse group of people and I was definitely intrigued. Then a guy about 50 years old appeared at the front of the altar and welcomed us. His name was Russ and he had shoulder length hair, full beard and kind eyes. He began by saying:

"Welcome and thank you for being here. This week is all about service and giving back. It is also a chance for each of you to deepen your spirituality and faith. Together we will explore who we are & the difference we can make in the lives of others. My name is Russ and I will be your tour guide throughout the week. We have some interesting things planned for each of you but most of all you will be put to work at the many non-profits we partner with. Each one of you will be assigned a place to work for the week and each evening we will come back here to the Church, break bread and talk about our experience. We have cots set up in the basement. This is where you will sleep. This is a week of fellowship and sharing, introspection and discovery and hard work. Today you are strangers but by the end of the week I believe you will all be good friends. We ask that you open yourself up to the experience and strive to be yourself. It is a safe place emotionally and we will treat one another with respect and compassion. Be ready to have a transformational experience!"

With the way I was feeling, this is what I needed to hear. I was searching for anything to help me thru this dark time. I think what I was truly looking for was HOPE. The next morning we awoke bright and early ready for our work assignments. We were going to be given an address to report to and that's all we knew. The rest would be revealed when we arrived at our work destination. I was given an envelope with where I was to go and I was supposed to get there by 8:30am. I opened my envelope and it read St. Gelasius Church at 64th & Woodlawn on the South side of Chicago.

"Please report to the building adjacent to the Church, St. Martin de Porres Shelter for Women & Children."

Now I knew where I'd be spending my week. I arrived at 8:20am and rang the bell. A rather robust African American woman opened the steel enforced door and said with a big smile,

"How can I help you?"

I introduced myself and told her that I was a volunteer and would be working there for the week. She welcomed me into the building and then welcomed me into her arms and gave me a very warm and caring hug. I immediately felt at ease. She said,

"Let me get the boss lady. She'll let you know what to do."

She went over to the phone, dialed an extension and said.

"Sister Therese, I have a young man here, Mr. Eddie and he is ready to work!"

Then I noticed a very diminutive white woman coming down the staircase. I remember thinking that this can't be Sr. Therese. I was thinking that she must be a big, strong and domineering woman to run a place like this but the woman coming down the stairs was 4'10 and probably about 90 pounds. She was tiny. She walked from the stairs directly to me and said with a warm smile,

"Welcome to the House of HOPE."

I had no idea it was known as *"The House of Hope"* but when she said those words I instantly felt a jolt of electricity rush thru me. I felt I was right where I needed to be. Sr. Therese showed me around the shelter while introducing me to the residents. The place was an old elementary school that had been turned into a shelter. It had many rooms to it amid 3 levels. She took me throughout the place pointing out the different rooms and what they represented. The first stop was the large communal eating area and kitchen. We then went to the television room, which was quite small. Next came the living room that was filled with bookshelves and comfy chairs and couches. Next she showed me the classroom where many of the shelters younger kids attended school. Then she brought me to the third level. This level had two rather large rooms that were filled wall to wall with bunk beds. It reminded me of an army barracks. Next to a few of the bunk beds were old wooden cribs. The rooms slept about 50 and they all shared a large communal bathroom. This bathroom was more like a locker room with several shower stalls amid many bathroom stalls. The lower level was simply a basement area where they kept all their storage and donations from clothing to toiletries to Christmas presents for the kids. After the tour, Sr. Therese sat me down and began to explain what the *"House of Hope"* was all about.

"Our shelter is like a family. We work with only women and their children who are in need and who are homeless. In fact, we cater to a specific demographic of the homeless population; all of our adult residents are recovering from addictions to drugs and or alcohol. More and more we find ourselves serving women who are suffering from mental illness, Post Traumatic stress disorder and chronic health issues. This sacred place has a nondiscriminatory policy in terms of disability, race and sexuality, religious or political affiliation. We do tend to serve primarily minorities. Our House of Hope has currently 53 residents. We have 26 women and 27 children. The kids range in age from three months to 16 years of age. When a person comes to us they are able to stay for up to one year until we get them functioning on their own. But we have had people stay longer if needed. Within that year we hope to have them clean and sober, working and able to become a contributing member of society. We do not have a lot of men that volunteer so you may feel a bit awkward with all this estrogen floating around. We encourage you to get to know the residents and just treat them, as you'd wish to be treated. Moreover, spend some time with the children. They are starving for love and affection and they rarely get to see many white men so you could possibly have a very positive influence. We will have you do various things throughout the week from cleaning, to cooking to helping us fix things. We will also have you help out in the school as an assistant to our teacher. If you ever have any questions or concerns, I am the one you should come to. We have some group time with the women where they talk about their story and share how they're doing. You are more than welcome to join us for that. Do you have any questions?"

I had many questions but I kept them to my self. Throughout that week I served where I was needed. The best thing about the week, were the relationships I'd made along the way. I came to learn the true courage of the residents in that program. I came to know who they were by listening to their personal stories. So much of what those women had been thru was truly heartbreaking. As I listened, I came to once again realize how the playing field of life was simply not equal. I know that seems obvious but it is astonishing when you hear it firsthand. The poverty, the lack of opportunity, the violence and the drugs that are so prevalent in their world are simply not a part of mine and as I listened I wondered how would I hold up in a similar existence? But their circumstance is not my circumstance and the more I learned about their world the words "There but for the Grace of God go I" entered my mind several times. It was then that I realized again how blessed I truly had been.

That week at that shelter had a deep impact on me because it changed my perspective. Perspective is the one thing we all need a healthy dose of from time to time. It can help us recognize what is good in our lives as opposed to what's not. One thing that was significant about that week was that at the end of it, I was no longer depressed. I was exhilarated and inspired to do more to serve others and I was committed to continue in some way to serve that shelter. I decided that later that winter, I would take the kids from the shelter sledding. So I did and it was a magical experience! Then in the summer I brought them to a park, bought a bunch of kites and had them fly kites while having a picnic. When one of the little 6 year old boys had a birthday, I brought them all to "Chuck E Cheeses" and celebrated his birthday there. One thing I am truly proud of is since 1993 I have held a Christmas Dance Party every year at the Shelter for a night of great food, fun and dancing! We cater in a wonderful dinner from the same place I catered the shelter back when I was in College: " Lee n' Eddie's." I bring volunteers and family members and friends and neighbors to help serve and run the party and many gifts and essentials are donated to the Mothers and Children for Christmas. I don't tell you this to impress you but rather to impress upon you the importance of service in our lives and the commitment we need to have to those we serve. I am proud to say that every person that has come with me to, "The House of Hope" will tell you how much they loved the experience at that magical place! To this day I am committed to giving back in whatever way I can to that beautiful place because when I needed them most at a very dark time in my life, they saved me. That commitment to service will not only benefit others who are in need but it will also serve your soul while providing your life a deeper purpose. Be careful though because this feeling can become addictive! I haven't missed a year in 28 years!!!

In the 2nd step of the four minute formula we talked about how if you want to attract something good or positive into your life you cannot talk or think about what is wrong or missing in your life. You must talk and think about how you want things to be. What this shift in perspective can do is get you to begin to channel your energies toward creating it. We have to be hyper vigilante about what we think about. Our thoughts become things. What we attach our focus towards becomes the basis of our experience. As Human beings it is within our nature to seek and discover and I believe we all have deeper questions about life. Who am I and why am I here? Our spiritual side is the part of us that can give our lives its most profound experiences. We must find ways to nurture and feed the spiritual side of our being. Service to others provides the nutrients and the fuel to our soul. It awakens us to the most beautiful and magnificent parts of our being.

The older I've become there is one spiritual study that became very intriguing to me: BUDDHISM. In Buddhism the answer to these questions is to be a "Buddha" which in sand script translates to mean FULLY AWAKE. One strives to be fully developed in all of the minds positive qualities and fully free of the negative ones. Take an acorn for example. The true nature of an acorn is to become an oak tree. That acorn could be used as a decoration, a piece of jewelry or even a weapon but it's true nature is to become an oak tree. If you give an acorn all the appropriate conditions it will become that oak tree. The true nature of our mind is to become free of clutter and negativity and be awake and positive. We are meant to be in an existence of total empathy with all living things. We are to understand that we are all those living things and they are all you. When we give ourselves all the right conditions then we will manifest our "True Nature" which is our oak tree. We need to first recognize the acorn in ourselves, and what we are meant to become.

I have really gravitated to the teachings of Buddhism because the practice of its teachings are truly empowering. In other words, the answers lie within us. Therefore, we are the answer! The root cause of all our suffering resides within our minds. There are surely external conditions for our suffering but the root cause according to the teachings of the Buddha is within what he calls our "Monkey Mind." The source for all our happiness is also within that same mind so the only way to truly free oneself from suffering is to understand and change our mind. One important point is understanding the true essence of the word "MIND." The "MIND" they speak of in Buddhism is not limited to our brains. Rather it is more then our brain, it is about the whole physical, mental, spiritual and emotional experience of being alive. It refers to something that encapsulates the whole experience of being alive. When we try to meditate and focus on an object like our breath, we diminish, at least for a time the opportunity for "disturbing thoughts" to enter our mind. This "practice" can be so vital. Think about a glass of water. When you shake the glass the water becomes shaken and disturbed much like our minds can become. When we stop shaking the glass and place it down it goes back to its natural state of stillness and calm and is now able to reflect things.

As negative thoughts come into our consciousness instead of trying to ignore or get rid of it we should first look at it, investigate it and try to understand it. Same thing with the things we deem positive in our lives. We should first look deeply into it and try to discover its origins. This deepening of awareness can help us understand how to live a more "mindful" life. This "mindfulness" can cause us to cease hurting ourselves, and others. It's amazing how much harm we bring upon ourselves without fully knowing or being aware that we are causing such pain and anxiety. This is why in the Buddhist philosophy one should never cling to conditions because they are always impermanent and changing. Just like in our lives. Learning to utilize conditions and not attaching to them can become a positive tool towards ones own liberation. We are hard wired to want to experience happiness yet we keep running into suffering. The path laid out in Buddhism is done so to help lead you toward your own happiness and fulfillment. For example, the path of leading an ethical and conscientious life is one that when practiced brings about a state of more happiness and fulfillment. The path of meditation is about settling the mind and being at peace so as to experience more serenity. It's not about suffering but rather fully understanding the suffering so as not to repeat it over and over again. It's in the practice that the revelations are made and the experience felt. We must take the time to be mindful of this each day, which in turn can create experiences of true happiness.

As my kids were growing up I wanted them to experience some other forms of spirituality besides Catholicism. I had been very attracted to and interested in Buddhism and so I thought this could be an interesting experience for the kids to experience and meet with a Buddhist monk. So I did a little research and low and behold there was a Buddhist temple about 10 miles from our home. I called and a lovely man picked up the phone. He said his name was Ajahn Peppercorn. I didn't know it then but "Ajahn" meant teacher. I told him of my interest in learning more about Buddhism and how I wanted my kids to experience meeting and learning from a Buddhist monk. He couldn't have been friendlier or more inviting when he graciously told us to come on by anytime. He told us that Tuesday's in the evening is a day of worship and if you come by around dinner before the worship he could speak with us. I was surprised that the man who answered the pho was the Buddhist monk himself. I told him "thank you" and that we would be by on Tuesday around 5pm. When I told my kids about the upcoming plan to visit the Buddhist temple they were confused and reluctant. I simply said it would be an interesting experience and one that I felt could enrich our lives. When Tuesday came around, we went.

When we arrived at the Temple, it wasn't a temple at all. It was a building that resembled an elementary school. There were a lot of people there celebrating some sort of occasion on the main level when we walked in. Then a short unassuming Asian man walked up and welcomed us in as though we were old friends. It was Ajahn Peppercorn. I introduced him to my wife and my two children and he couldn't have been sweeter. He invited us to follow him to an upper level of the building where we walked into a worship sanctuary with large Pillows and an elevated but tiny altar. Ajahn instructed us to grab 4 pillows and sit before the altar. He excused himself and said he'd be right back. A few minutes passed as we sat adjacent to one another on the floor atop the large pillows. When Ajahn reappeared he had on a beautiful flowing robe as he sat upon the little altar right in front of us. He then simply said,

"How can I help you today?"

I asked if he would be willing to tell us a bit about Buddhism and what it means to be a Buddhist. He smiled a very peaceful smile and simply began talking. The following is an overview of what my family and I learned on that day. I share this with you because it is a day that I will never forget and it has served me in ways that I am grateful for everyday!

He started with some of the history of Buddhism and its origins. How it began around 480BC in a beautiful palace in Nepal. The Buddha came into this world as a child of great wealth and privilege and his name was Siddharta Gautama. When he was born, an old hermit acetic came to the palace where they allowed him to see and hold the newborn and he informed them that their son will become a great emperor If he stays within the confines of the Palace but if he ventures out he will be a great spiritual leader of the World. His Father, who was the King decided to keep him sequestered and protected so that he too would become a great Emperor. He was catered to and kept within the Palace and every desire and want was available to him. He was taught to see the world as flawless and opulent. He wasn't aware that pain, aging or death even existed. At age 16 he was married and the world was his oyster. Then one day he convinced his Father that if he was to be a great emperor then he needed to see more of the world. His Father, who after 29 years had kept him sequestered, figured that his son could not be swayed by anything he saw out in the world so he permitted him to go. At 29 years old Siddharta ventured out into the world.

At first he was enchanted by what he was seeing. The World was so vast and different from the Palace and all its lavishness. It was real and simply amazing! Then one day he stumbled upon a man who was coughing. Now you need to understand that Siddharta had been sheltered from all things and he had never been sick. He didn't even know what that was. He inquired to the man coughing as to what was wrong and the man explained that he was ill. Siddharta did not know that could happen to someone and it was very eye opening and shocking to him. On his second trip out into the Kingdom Siddharta came across an old man. He had never seen anyone so aged before and he didn't know because of his sheltering that we all become old. Then on another excursion out into the world, Siddharta came across a dead body. Siddharta had never seen death before and again had no idea this could happen. This shook Siddharta to his core. He became very depressed now knowing that everyone he loved would one day become sick, old and would die. This was a very trying time for the young man. He decided to head out into the Kingdom again to take a long walk and try and process what he now knew. On this walk, Siddharta came across a homeless man who was very poor yet full of joy and peace and happiness. This homeless man had renounced all material things and was on a spiritual quest to escape all of life's sufferings. This was the most perplexing of all to Siddharta because he could not believe a person in such awful circumstances could be so joyful. But the man was genuinely happy. This had opened Siddharta eyes for the first time as to the way life truly was and he realized in that moment how little he knew. Thus, Siddharta decided that he had to leave the palace his Wife and newborn Son to venture out into the world to find an answer to life's suffering. Thus, he began his quest and a whole new experience of life awaited him.

His first encounter was with five ascetics living in the woods who practiced extreme deprivation to achieve enlightenment. Siddharta joined these ascetics and began a six-year fast, exposed to the elements and ate

nothing but the seeds that fell into his lap. After suffering extreme deprivation and coming very close to death several times, he realized all this did
was make him weak and his mind slow due to the starvation and he knew
in his heart this could not be the path to enlightenment. He gave up his
fast and immediately began to nourish himself. He believed the answer
was not in extreme deprivation or extreme indulgence which he had experienced both in abundance. He realized the answer must fall somewhere in
between the two. (Thus came the seeds of the "middle path" which would
become the Buddha's major teaching.) After Siddharta left the ascetics he
wandered until he found a Bodhi tree (fig tree) that he would sit under and
meditate until he had reached enlightenment. He sat under that tree for 49
days and became the enlightened one, the "Buddha."

The story was fascinating and the way Ajahn told it with such passion and pleasure, it really pulled us in. He went on to share with us where
the enlightenment had led the Buddha. He came to understand and teach
are what's known as the 4 Noble truths:

Truth #1: Life is suffering. No matter what you do in life, you're going
to suffer. Ultimately everyone grows old, gets sick and dies. (Remember
the encounters he had when he left the palace for the first time)

Truth #2: We suffer because of our craving. We become attached
to impermanent things and because of this we are destined to suffer. We
need to learn to be happy with what we have instead of longing for what
we don't have.

Truth #3: We can escape the cycle of suffering.

Truth #4: The noble 8-fold path can help us escape suffering and
achieve enlightenment! The noble 8-fold path is what's known as "THE
MIDDLE WAY." It lies between the indulgences of a young prince and the
deprivation of the ascetic.

So what is this 8-fold path?

It is what the Buddha not only lived by but also taught wherever he
went. It is basically 8 guidelines by which to live ones life. The 8-fold path

is not to be done in order but rather like a wheel you spin as you contemplate certain situations of your life. Remember though that it is a path, a way in which to experience your life. By following this path it can lead you to Nirvana & Enlightenment. I share this with you in this final chapter because I believe it can help guide you on your journey to live your best life. This is not religion nor spirituality but rather a way in which to conduct yourself along your journey. Let's take a look at these 8 steps.

Step 1: Right view (understanding)

This is the viewpoint and understanding that the 4 noble truths can help you stop suffering. We need to realize that everything in this world is impermanent.

Step 2: Right intent

Why are you doing things? What is motivating the choices and behaviors of your life? If things are done out of anger they will lead to suffering. If things are done out of love they will alleviate suffering.

Step 3: Right speech

Words matter. What we say to others has an impact. We should never hurt others with the things we say. When we do, it obviously adds suffering to the world. Not being deceptive is a major part of this step. When we lie to ourselves and to others it creates suffering. Gossip falls into this category. When we gossip it adds to the misery and pain of the world. We should strive to be truthful & honest always and not just with others but with ourselves.

Step 4: Right action

We should always strive to do "good" with our actions. Do not act in a way that is negative. This step covers the "5 precepts" which is akin to the Buddhist 10 commandments (although there's only 5) They are:

-Do not harm any living creatures

-Do not steal

-Do not engage in sexual misconduct

-Do not lie or hurt people with words

-Do not take intoxicating substances.

Step 5: Right livelihood

We should earn our living in an honest and ethical way. We shouldn't be involved in shady dealings or anything to do with crime, arms, drugs, usury of people i.e. Slave trade, which was something the Buddha was very much against.

Step 6: Right effort

In all things you do you should do to the best of your ability and with honor. Whether you are at work, cleaning a dish, making a bed or playing with your children. You need to be mindful of the best effort you can give to each task. Going about this with positivity will help enhance the quality of the experience.

Step 7: Right mindfulness

Be present and in the moment. Whatever you are doing, make sure your mind and heart are right there with you. While walking along the beach be mindful of the sand between your toes, the sounds of the surf the air in your lungs. Do not be walking on the beach thinking about something bad that happened to you years ago or about a person who wronged you back then. Do not walk along that beach wishing you had a boat. Be grateful for the moment you are experiencing NOW and be present. You may have negative fleeting thoughts, just don't attach to it and let it drift out of mind like the clouds across the sky and come back to the moment.

Step 8: Right concentration

We need to focus our minds in order to see things for how they truly are. We need to practice thru meditation by being able to focus on a single object or concept without distraction. This concentration of mind can help us follow thru with proper behaviors and actions.

By following this path you can reach the state of "Nirvana." When you are able to extinguish from your life all wants and desires you too can reach enlightenment. This is a tough thing to do when we come from the western world where the acquisition of things is a primary way of life. Imagine a life of just being and not wanting. It could be incredibly liberating and may just open yourself up to your true essence.

As we come to the end of our journey together, I hope that this book and my "Four Minute Formula" has given you some insights and concrete ways in which to live your life to the best of your ability! Being a "PEAK PERFORMANCE" expert I have spent close to 30 years teaching, speaking, consulting, coaching and advising people from all walks of life on how to do just that. This book took over a decade to write because this "Formula" took time to evolve into what you've just experienced. In the end, we each will have many destinations but without a doubt the fullness and abundance of our lives is experienced in the journey. This is your journey! Right here and right now! Live it to the best of your ability with Authenticity, Compassion, Empathy, Forgiveness, Gratitude, Hope & Love! As I say "Good Bye" may I also say "THANK YOU" for allowing me to be a part of your Journey. I wish you all PEACE as you move forward striving to live YOUR BEST LIFE!!!

ONE LAST TIME: "THE FOUR MINUTE FORMULA"

1. DECIDE WHAT YOU WANT & WHY

2. BELIEVE

3. IDENTIFY YOUR TEAM

4. CREATE THE GAME PLAN

5. PREPARE FOR THE PAIN

6. SET YOUR DESTINATION POINT

7. GIVE BACK TO THE WORLD